The Art and Science of Leading

What Effective Administrators Understand

Second Edition

Peter Lorain

ROWMAN & LITTLEFIELD
Lanham • Boulder • New York • London

Published by Rowman & Littlefield
A wholly owned subsidiary of The Rowman & Littlefield Publishing Group, Inc.
4501 Forbes Boulevard, Suite 200, Lanham, Maryland 20706
www.rowman.com

Unit A, Whitacre Mews, 26-34 Stannary Street, London SE11 4AB

Copyright © 2016 by Peter Lorain

All rights reserved. No part of this book may be reproduced in any form or by any electronic or mechanical means, including information storage and retrieval systems, without written permission from the publisher, except by a reviewer who may quote passages in a review.

British Library Cataloguing in Publication Information Available

Library of Congress Cataloging-in-Publication Data

Names: Lorain, Peter, 1943-
The art and science of leading : what effective administrators understand / Peter Lorain.
Description: Lanham, Maryland : Rowman and Littlefield, [2016] | Includes bibliographical references.
Identifiers: LCCN 2016003989 (print) | LCCN 2016013275 (ebook) | ISBN 9781475826173 (cloth : alk. paper) | ISBN 9781475826180 (pbk. : alk. paper) | ISBN 9781475826197 (Electronic)
Subjects: LCSH: Educational leadership--United States. | School administrators--United States. | School management and organization--United States.
Classification: LCC LB2805 .L56 2016 (print) | LCC LB2805 (ebook) | DDC 371.2--dc23 LC record available at http://lccn.loc.gov/2016003989

∞ ™ The paper used in this publication meets the minimum requirements of American National Standard for Information Sciences Permanence of Paper for Printed Library Materials, ANSI/NISO Z39.48-1992.

Printed in the United States of America

Contents

Foreword		ix
Preface		xi
Acknowledgments		xiii
Introduction		xv
1	Art and Science	1
2	Understand the Gestalt: Everything Affects Everything	3
3	A Set of Leadership Tenets	9
4	Leadership: Definition and Beliefs	11
	Unintended Influence/Conscious Behavior	11
	Influential Leadership	12
	Productive Leadership	13
	Beliefs and Values	14
	Formal and Informal Leadership	18
	Getting Something Done	19
5	Effective, Exemplary Leaders	21
	Change	23
	Formal Preparation	27
	Mentors	27
	Natural or Innate Ability	28
	Experience Enhances Future Performance	29
6	Instructional Leadership	31
	Leaders Have a Vision	33
	Realizing the Vision	34
	Working with People Is Inherent in Leadership	34
	All the Time	36
	Working with a Variety of Processes	37
	Preparation	37
7	The Age of Standards: Implications for Effective Leadership	39
	Gary Sehorn	
	A Bigger Stage	39
	The Shifting Locus of Control	39
	Administrators as Translators and Interpreters	40
	Fidelity and School Mission	41
	Schooling as a Marketplace	41

	Defining Success	42
	Communities as Full Partners	42
	Creating Space for the Art and Science of School Leadership	43
8	Management	45
	Safe and Orderly Environment	45
	Protect the Investment	47
	The Facility as a Safe Environment	47
	Impressions Are Important	48
9	Intentional, Analytic Decision Making	51
10	Delegating	57
	To Whom to Delegate	58
	Effective Delegation	61
	Micromanaging, or Rather, *Not* Micromanaging	62
11	Analysis Prior to Decision Making	67
	Decisions—Everything Still Affects Everything	70
	An Error or a Mistake?	74
12	Elements of Leadership	77
	Getting Back to People	77
	Valuing Instincts	79
	Communication Is Critical: Written, Spoken, Interpersonal	81
	Knowing When to Act . . . and When to Wait	82
	Being Objective	82
	The Courage to Do What's Right	83
	Organization to Get Things Done	83
13	Goals: Planning, Organizational, Individual	87
	Strategic Planning	87
	Organizational Goals	89
	Sources of Institutional Goals	92
	Individual Goal Setting	92
	Helping Others	94
14	Power	97
15	Meetings and Agendas	101
	Kinds of Meetings	101
	Reasons for Meetings	102
	Leadership Roles	104
	Who Conducts Meetings	104
	Fundamental Skills	105
	An Art	106
	Reacting to Documents	108
	Agendas	109
	How Are These Abilities Acquired?	110

16 Future Leaders: A Program to Identify, Recruit, and
Prepare Prospective Administrative Leaders   113
Mike Scott
    Future Leaders   113
    Identifying Potential Participants   114
    What It Is   115
    What It Isn't   116
    Elements and Content of the Program   116

17 The Administrative Interview   119
    The Three Steps of Preparation   121

18 Time to Reflect and Recharge: Valuing Vacations   127

19 The Gestalt of Leadership   129

Conclusion   131
    Differences   134
    Volunteers   135
    Fiscal and Legal Knowledge   138
    The National Middle School Association Search   139
    Summary   140

Appendix 1   141
    Strategic Plan Outline   141

Appendix 2   145
    National Association of Secondary School Principals'
    (NASSP) Assessment Center   145

References   147

About the Authors   149

Foreword

I first met Peter Lorain in the early 1970s when I was a scruffy, quiet high school sophomore and he was my "groovy" counselor. It was no ordinary suburban high school. Patterned after an experimental school in nearby Portland, it was an open and student-centered laboratory for a cluster of cutting-edge educational theories. Students and teachers were on a first name basis. Students and teachers alike shared the faculty lounge and the adjacent smoking court. The campus was open, the rules were few, and the student body had just one tradition: no traditions! Pete experienced the high water mark of the experimentation, and the pendulum swing back to a more traditional approach to schooling.

Pete's presence in that setting—edgy, experimental reforms in the 1960s and 1970s and their aftermath—is an example of a fascinating feature of his career. Since Pete loves movies, it's only fitting to illustrate this aspect of his career through film. The title character in *Forrest Gump* manages to accidentally be present at a number of iconic historical moments. In Forrest Gump fashion, Pete has been a part of many significant moments and movements in recent educational history, but unlike the film's character, Pete's presence has not been accidental. His success and the recognition of his leadership put him there. He has been a leader at all levels over the past four decades, a time marked by dramatic changes in public education.

Beginning as a high school teacher, he moved into counseling, became a building administrator, then a central office administrator and a leader in a national association. His leadership in middle level education came just as junior high schools became outdated and middle schools were established as the new norm across the country. Along the way, he had a role in local, state, and national level leadership. Pete writes, "An effective leader exists within a milieu, a total environment. Within that milieu, leadership behavior and decision-making is a gestalt." That gestalt benefits me, as one of the many who have had the advantage of Pete's mentorship, and this book will spread that benefit to many more.

Leadership is a slippery concept, but Pete focuses on two pillars: change and complexity. He presents a leadership framework informed by a career that has traversed a constantly changing milieu. His examples span the levels of his own experience and demonstrate how consistent values can be maintained in the midst of change. His ability to read people and situations is uncanny, and his insightful analyses combine with his wit to make him a voice that is worthy of attention.

As a young administrator, I had the chance to join Pete as his vice principal in a large, successful junior high. I was part of the leadership team he directed as the district adopted the middle school model, and I clung to his coattails as he assumed an active role in the middle school movement at both the state and national levels. From that point on, I have had the benefit of his guidance and example. Pete is a careful and considerate analyst, both participating in and critiquing educational change and leadership. His own leadership is marked by integrity, and he understands the difference between influence and authority. Unsentimental about most things, he "gets" people—what makes them tick and why they behave as they do—and he is a humanist to the core who is deeply concerned about people. Coupled with his care for others is a clear-eyed realism about the truths of leadership.

Pete does not sail, but he's expertly navigated the waters of educational leadership for decades. He looks beyond the sudden squalls and surface waves to the larger weather patterns and deep currents. He has a steady hand and a strong ethical rudder and keeps his well-trained eye on the horizon. There's little Pete hasn't seen out on those turbulent waters. If you are trying to navigate the waters of educational leadership, as you read through this book I encourage you to envision yourself on a bar stool at a harborside tavern listening in as the wise captain next to you shares his leadership insights and observations. Knowing Pete, I'm sure he'd buy a round!

Gary Sehorn

Preface

In the spring of 2013, three friends, all leaders in education, were enjoying their quarterly lunch and get-together. The three had known each other for years and worked together in the same school, then worked together in the same district in positions different from when they were together in the same school. They also had been significantly involved in the state middle school association. All three had been successful administrators at both the building and district levels.

Currently, they were taking their work in education in three different directions. One was superintendent of a large school district; another was a professor in the school of education at a small private university. The third member of the lunch group, among many other projects for the association, had recently chaired and completed an executive director search for National Middle School Association, now Association for Middle Level Education.

The conversation at lunch was interesting and enjoyable. During lunch they told the old stories and remembered the people involved in them. They discussed the state of education and current issues and trends. They updated each other on their current work and the aspects of their projects and undertakings.

At one point in the conversation, Gary, the university professor, asked the third member of the group, "As you conducted the searches for the executive director position, where did you find the best candidates? Where did they come from? What is the best preparation for a position like that?"

Gary was adamant, though his friend laughed it off after a moment's thought and quick response. Then Gary said, "I'm holding you to this!" At that, the friend agreed to put something in writing. He said he would attempt to answer the questions in a thoughtful, helpful way.

At first, his writing began to respond directly to the question. However, after thinking about the many qualities that were desirable and needed in an executive director, ones that included a wide range of leadership qualities and behaviors, the writing became stalled. Before addressing "from where and what background" it became necessary to first identify "What is a leader in education? Who is that person and what does that person look like? What qualities and skills and background go into the making of an effective leader?"

Those leadership questions are the ones that the first edition, *The Gestalt of Leadership: A Handbook for Leaders in Education*, answered. This second edition, *The Art and Science of Leading: What Effective Administrators Understand*, expands on that book. Using *The Gestalt* as the foundation, *The Art and Science* updates the earlier work and adds significant new information.

The following pages contain a story. Others who would write and teach about leadership may add to, delete some, or substitute parts of the material shared here. Each person's path to leadership is unique, and I hope that *The Art and Science of Leading* contains and provides information, concepts, and advice that support any leader's goals and development and help further the leadership journey.

Acknowledgments

Leadership development is cumulative. I was fortunate to know and work with wonderful, profound, exceptional leaders during my education and in my career. Along the way, I studied leadership writing, documents, and assessments. To that I added what I learned and observed from those outstanding leaders. I was merely the penman for most of them.

Schools are filled with many excellent teachers, like high school teachers Miss Ogata and Mrs. Davidson.

Throughout college and graduate university experiences I continued to learn about and define leadership. I worked with several excellent professors, including Warren Pickett as an undergraduate as well as the entire graduate counselor education department at the University of Pittsburgh.

I have known and worked with many fine, and some not so fine, school administrators. Dell Squire, a high school principal when I worked with him, later a superintendent, was a personal mentor.

Associations are fortunate to have so many dedicated educators working with them, and I respect and am in admiration of the work they do in the state and national arena. I worked alongside many of these wonderful and bright people, people like Sue Swaim, former executive director of the National Middle School Association, now the Association for Middle Level Education. We learned from each other—at least I learned from them.

There are five people without whom this book never would have been written.

- Gary Sehorn and Mike Scott, two friends, colleagues, lunch companions, and contributors to this second edition. They were the ones who asked the question. Gary was even a little adamant.
- Micki Casley, a university professor and administrator and award-winning researcher. Micki was gracious enough to read an early, early edition (a rather poor one), and contribute her editing expertise. After sharing her ideas and edits, she said, "This is a book."
- Nothing I have done in the past thirty-five years has been without the unconditional love, support, and encouragement from Jan Burgess, including this second edition, which she patiently and critical-

ly read, once again, and made important idea contributions. Educator. Published author. Friend and companion. Wife.
- Finally, I have read a lot of books, all of which contain "acknowledgments." The acknowledgment page almost always includes a thank-you to the publisher and editor, and I wondered why always the sincere, glowing words. I now know. I have to thank Thomas Koerner at Rowman & Littlefield.

Tom received the first copy of the manuscript and, in spite of its being less than impressive, he read it. He must have seen potential, as he was encouraging and provided helpful critique. He shared ideas for additional content, content that he thought would be helpful to the intended audience. After reading those changes and, once again, the manuscript, he said, "I like what I am reading."

A year later he suggested an update under a different title. That suggestion became this second edition, *The Art and Science of Leading: What Effective Administrators Understand*.

Without his support, encouragement, and willingness to look at and develop "what could be," I would not have continued.

A special thank-you to Paul Simon and his music, music that has inspired and spoken to and for so many of us over the years.

The Boxer
Words & Music by Paul Simon
© Copyright 1968 Paul Simon (BMI)
All Rights Reserved. International Copyright Secured.
Used by Permission.

Introduction

The genesis and inspiration for writing *The Gestalt of Leadership* was a series of questions from colleagues about effective school and executive association leadership. It was read and found to be useful by a much broader audience, which supported the contention that leadership skills and beliefs are universal. A member of a church board of elders found the material on group dynamics as written in "Influential Leadership" to be very helpful in understanding and participating in that role. A private health care provider used the "Strategic Planning" model to create and realize a vision for his clinic.

This second edition, *The Art and Science of Leading: What Effective Administrators Understand,* narrows the focus to school leadership, with the conclusion addressing the executive director questions and role. Both editions were set in an educational context, written as (1) a guide, (2) a resource, and (3) a professional development tool. They were written with schools and school leadership personnel as the potential audience.

Specifically, this second edition was written with the idea that it might:

- Be a critical and significant contribution to existing administrators (or anyone) in assessing their leadership and planning their own personal professional growth and development
- Provide a resource for college and university professors engaged in the preparation and education of future educational leaders and administrators
- Inform and guide educators who are curious about or preparing for a career in administration
- Be a resource for existing administrators who are formally or informally serving as mentors to prospective administrators
- Contribute to the study of leadership and leadership in education

Like *The Gestalt of Leadership*, *The Art and Science of Leading* is both conceptual and practical. It contains several theories and components of effective and exemplary leadership. It then provides real-life examples to illustrate those theories. Although a few of the examples contain fictional elements, virtually all of them come from the experiences of the author or events and people that he has known or with whom he has worked.

Occasionally, an administrator is quoted though there is no reference or name attributed to the statement. These quotations may be based on comments from actual individuals; however, they are listed as quotations for dialogue purposes only and intended to reflect the essence of the conversation and not to be a direct quote. The actual comment or quotation would be similar, but not exactly like that included in the example.

One challenge in writing a book about people is the lack of an English-language gender-neutral pronoun. Exemplary leaders are both women and men. To avoid the stilted "he/she" and "him/her" construction, you will see both male and female pronouns used interchangeably. Know that these circumstances are equally applicable to both men and women.

Whether for personal professional growth or as a resource for others aspiring to administration, perhaps this book will be helpful to anyone interested in education and providing leadership as educators work to realize the mission: to educate all children so they all may become thoughtful, independent, successful, and happy adults—ones who make positive contributions to the well-being of their community, their country, and their world.

ONE
Art and Science

Art: a skill in performance acquired by experience, study, or observation. Human ingenuity in adapting natural things to man's use. Systematic application of knowledge or skill in effecting a desired result (*Webster's*).

Science: possession of knowledge; something that must be studied or learned; a system or method based on or purporting to be based on scientific principles (*Webster's*).

The Art and Science of Leading is grounded in these two critical elements.

All professions have a knowledge base and set of skills that can be taught, learned, and applied (science). In the hands of some, those fundamental components meld over time and elevate the practice into a highly effective form (art). This is also true in leadership.

Bodies of knowledge are accessible through coursework, reading, and professional development activities. An effective administrative leader will have a thorough knowledge base regarding issues, contexts, and processes of leadership in education. That is the *science.*

The most effective administrative leaders have the ability to apply that knowledge base to people, institutions, and situations. That is, the *art* and the degree to which it can be applied will many times determine the degree of success. Several examples are outlined below:

- *Science*: A teacher who knows the format for an effective lesson uses target learning goals. *Art*: That teacher implements the lesson with attention to students' conceptual understanding, readiness, interest, and grasp of the material.
- *Science*: A principal knows the policy and procedure regarding teacher evaluation. *Art*: The principal implements that knowledge collaboratively based on a teacher's strengths, interests, personal

goals, and needs and shares ideas and examples that are enriching and measurable.
- *Science*: A teacher understands that an essential concept needs activities that match and lead students to understanding. *Art*: That teacher is aware of students' progress and provides scaffolding activities at key points, knowing and allowing students' interests to be a part of the reinforcement activities.
- *Science*: An administrator knows that there is a need to set leadership team goals aligned to school-wide learning goals and the school climate and does so. *Art*: The administrator works in collaboration with the team, assesses progress, provides and accepts feedback based on interests and data, monitors group dynamics as well as goal attainment, and adjusts and intervenes with support materials, encouragement, and participation when appropriate.
- *Science*: A superintendent knows the importance of having an organizational chart that lists positions. He knows that the budget supports all positions and that they must be filled. *Art*: That superintendent knows the strengths and needs of the district, the overall administrative team including the district-level administrative team, and each individual building. The superintendent makes appointments and hires so that each position and person complements the entire team and meets the needs of the district and building.

Throughout *The Art and Science of Leading: What Effective Administrators Understand*, there will be discussion of the science of administrative leadership. There will also be discussion of several intangibles such as instincts, inherent ability, and application—the art! In some cases, the science and art elements will be identified. In others, they are left to the reader.

The book will provide concepts, theories, needed skills, practical application techniques, and tools. Knowing each of these is critical to effective leadership. So is understanding them as a whole and applying them appropriately.

Just as every artist, like every piece of art, is unique, so is every administrative leader. Artists and administrative leaders will observe, interpret, and apply their knowledge, talent, personality, and unique outlook to the artistic work. For the administrator, that is the school. The administrator's individual uniqueness, for better or for worse, will become a part of the school. He will have impacted it in his own way and become a part of it. The goal is to do so in a way that leads to successful schools for all students.

TWO
Understand the Gestalt

Everything Affects Everything

> *Gestalt*: A structure or configuration of physical, biological, or psychological phenomena so integrated as to constitute a functional unit with properties not derivable from its parts in summation (*Webster's*).
>
> *Milieu*: Environment; setting (*Webster's*).

What follows in this chapter is a conceptual framework and philosophy, one that works for many administrators and leaders. The goals of these leaders are to enhance and maximize the personal success of others, to shape and influence outcomes, and to realize the mission of education.

Each separate factor that constitutes a person and a situation is an entity of its own, forming a composite—a *whole*. That whole is the gestalt.

Leadership does not and decisions do not occur in a vacuum or as separate, unconnected activities. The wise leader will have as complete as possible an understanding of virtually *everything* in relation to a situation for which a response is required.

The gestalt of leadership is a combination of all factors associated with the leadership event. A leader is a combination of experience, skills, abilities, instincts, training, and everything that contributes to that person's abilities. The gestalt of leadership is to take all of that and, considering the milieu (the numerous elements in the total environment), apply it to a situation, issue, or decision. Each of those factors from both the leader and the milieu will have an impact on all the others, making each decision and every day unique, different from the ones before it and the ones yet to come.

Because there are so many factors and variables affecting each other, there can be no one template for effective leadership. It is not possible to develop a protocol, overlay it onto a situation with its own unique conditions, and have a ready-made, prescriptive course of action.

Unless leadership is taking place within a controlled environment for the purposes of scientific study, every leadership experience will be unique. Each person will have different skills and backgrounds. The milieu—populations, history, climate—will vary. Situations and decisions will be altered as a result of new and changing issues and people. Attitudes and sensitivities of both the leader and the people involved can fluctuate from day to day. The sheer variety of elements impacts every aspect of effective leadership and each one will affect all the others.

To examine leadership, everything related to the experience must be considered. As many variables as possible must be factored in:

- The person who is in the authority position
- The backgrounds, expertise, experiences of everyone involved, not only of the person formally assigned as leader but also those who are influencing the process and outcome
- The issues being addressed and the conditions around them as well as the conditions in the milieu
- Short-term solutions to long-term possibilities and implications (analysis can help determine the balance of these two elements)
- The person to whom the leader reports and is accountable, formally or informally
- Social conditions, personal philosophies, and beliefs of everyone involved

All of these variables, virtually *everything*, come together to create a situation and condition where leadership, either successful or unsuccessful, will surface. To make things even more interesting, what "is" today will not be the same tomorrow. Because life and conditions and attitudes and new information and perceptions are fluid and dynamic, they all affect each other and they change from day to day. As a result, today's leadership behavior and decision may or may not be the same or appropriate tomorrow.

A single day is a short time span, but as days go by, the differences and changes will be more pronounced, which will result in a completely different milieu and thus a different analysis, decision, or behavior.

Examples are endless. A leader can apply the continuum analysis model formally and intuitively to virtually every decision to identify and consciously consider the *gestalt*—the whole.

Following are three approaches that illustrate a hiring situation. There are several commonalities to each approach. The same person is making the decision in all three examples; however, every situation contains variables, ones that affect each other. With each one the leadership experience varies, making the leadership gestalt different in each case.

Approach 1: In a particular school the principal always hired the staff. For subject matter positions he did all the screening and initial interviewing. He selected two or three teachers who would be good teachers and staff members. However, he also wanted the subject matter specialists involved. They were the ones who knew the content and could confirm that each candidate had the expected level of expertise and subject matter knowledge.

The incumbents, the teachers already on staff, were the ones who would work day to day with whomever was selected. The principal asked the department head or others in the department to interview each finalist and recommend one to the principal. The principal then conducted one final interview before finalizing the position.

That is one set of circumstances and is an example of one kind of leadership gestalt. Here's another using the same person in a leadership role.

Approach 2: The principal knew that his instincts and abilities to hire staff were good, including hiring other administrators. The principal was promoted to high school/middle school director and then again to personnel director. That same former principal was in a position to hire, or to influence the hiring teachers and other staff, even though the direct interviewing and hiring process was being carried out by the building- or other district-level administrators. He did have input, and he did interview most of the applicants who were being considered seriously. He was involved in hiring; however, in staffing schools (in most cases) he allowed the principals to make their hiring decisions.

This personnel director may have wanted but did not have the final decision in making selections for principalships or other district-level staff. That decision rested with the superintendent, and the superintendent may have had other ideas, been looking for specific skills, and had "favorites." In addition to the personnel director's preference and choice, and in addition to the superintendent's final decision, there were other invested constituent groups to consider: teachers, classified staff, and parents. Each of these groups desired, and deserved, a voice in the selection.

Even though the director believed he could have made good, and in some cases better, selections if he had been making the decision on his own, other people were involved in the process. He was at a lower authoritative decision-making level than was the superintendent, who had the final decision and applied his own instincts, preferences, biases, and experience to the selection.

This is a second example of the gestalt of leadership and decision making within the same general category—hiring. The situations, the people, the elements . . . everything is different and each one affects the others. Yet both approaches have the same goal and result in the same outcome—hiring of staff.

Here's one more.

Approach 3: As the chair of a search committee, a committee that was generating and vetting candidates, the task from the president and board was to recommend candidates for an executive director for a national association. This same former principal, the one who became a district office administrator and was an association volunteer, had several factors to consider, groups to involve, and needs to be met:

- The board, staff, and other association leaders had a stake in the selection process and final decision. In the case of the board, his role was to facilitate and use his influence as the board and search committee worked through the process and made the selection.
- The association staff clearly had an interest in the outcome and desired representation in the process and selection.
- There were members of other constituent groups (e.g., past officers, previous staff, affiliate leaders) who desired a role, or at least had an expectation to provide input.

In almost all cases, as the chair of the committee with past experience in teacher and administrator searches and hiring, having provided input for past searches, the chair thought he could accurately predict what the input would be. Indeed, prior to the initiation of the search, some input had already been considered and then factored in. Nonetheless, it was important to contact members of these groups so that they felt involved and their voices and preferences were included.

In every one of these three hiring scenarios there were common factors:

- The same person was involved in each example as a leader and either administrator or chair.
- Constituent and interested groups—incumbent teachers and department heads, teachers, classified staff, parents, board members, interest and pressure groups—brought their individual and collective personalities, beliefs, experience, and values to be considered, and they expected and deserved to be heard.

Though the factors were common, the coming together of those factors was entirely different and created an entirely different set of dynamics. The other formal leaders were different in each case, as were those who influenced the process and decision. As such, the leadership gestalt changed with each one. Though the general categories were the same in each example—the task was hiring; each group had leadership, both formal and informal; there were other groups involved—every specific issue within these general categories was different, and each one affected the others. This meant that each process required and produced very different leadership gestalts.

THREE
A Set of Leadership Tenets

Exemplary: Deserving of imitation; commendable (*Webster's*).

Milieu: Environment; setting (*Webster's*).

Effective leaders don't just sit down and say, "Maybe I'll become a leader someday," or, "I'll get involved because someday I'll receive an award." Effective leaders develop as they respond to situations and circumstances in the best way they know how in an attempt to "make things better." Although some individuals are born into lifestyles and an expectation that they one day will be in leadership positions and they are raised to meet that expectation, initially most effective leaders are developing and growing as they are just "being themselves."

Some people simply and naturally find themselves in leadership roles and positions; they exhibit traits that cause others to listen or follow. They know when to contribute, when to intervene, when to take charge, when to be thoughtful, and when to do nothing. Usually it is after they have found themselves in leadership roles that they begin to think about, develop, and take advantage of their abilities.

Leadership is a topic that has been researched, written about, and explored in all its dimensions and definitions. Yet no single work completely satisfies the student looking for a definitive piece that leads to effective leadership. In fact, one might suspect that it is impossible to read the studies and through that reading become an effective leader. The study is the science. Leadership requires the art.

The following list is a set of beliefs about leadership for anyone in formal and informal leadership positions:

- Exemplary leaders make things better.
- Exemplary leaders make people successful.

- There are natural leaders, authoritative leaders, knowledgeable and learned leaders. Exemplary leaders are a combination.
- Exemplary leaders also are a combination of "born" and "made." An exemplary leader cannot *just* be "made."
- Many leaders can be effective, but not all effective leaders are exemplary.
- Leadership is a gestalt.
- Leaders must be aware of the milieu and how it changes.
- Instructional and managerial leadership are both required in any educational organization.
- Not all decisions involve everyone, and different kinds of decisions require different input and from different sources.
- Nothing is "either/or." Everything is somewhere in between, and decisions and actions fall somewhere on a continuum that warrants consideration.

Leadership, schooling, association, and organization work implies "groups" of people. In every group there exists a variety of talents, skills, backgrounds, knowledge, and other assets, all of which are valuable and contribute to the whole. When considering the whole of a group, one particularly interesting consideration is the contribution of introverts and extroverts.

Susan Cain (2013) has written an insightful and defining book, *Quiet: The Power of Introverts in a World That Can't Stop Talking*, related to introversion, extroversion, and personality/leadership implications.

Introverts and extroverts possess unique characteristics, behaviors, tendencies, inclinations, and predispositions. They are also leaders whose predispositions and personalities significantly affect their leadership style and effectiveness. Consider a few points from *Quiet*:

- An introvert, as a member of a group of people, one who by definition may prefer to work alone, can be just as effective in developing project outcomes as a group, and in some cases, more effective.
- Quiet leadership is still leadership.
- Many introverts are successful and know how to behave and act in groups. Many extroverts have difficulties being alone.

Cain's fascinating book on introverts and extroverts has significant implications for a discussion of leadership because it establishes the fact that all of us are born with certain potentials and capacities. It also establishes that quiet, introverted leaders can be just as effective as outgoing and extroverted ones.

FOUR
Leadership
Definition and Beliefs

Leadership: The position or function of a leader, a person who guides or directs a group; administration, management, directorship, control, governorship, stewardship, hegemony, influence, command, effectiveness; sway, clout. An act or instance of leading; guidance; direction (Dictionary.com).

Continuum: 1. Something in which a fundamental common character is discernible amid a series of insensible or indefinite variations uniting discrete parts. 2. A continuous series or whole, no part of which is perceptibly different from the adjacent parts (Dictionary.com).

UNINTENDED INFLUENCE/CONSCIOUS BEHAVIOR

Expanding on the definition above, leadership can be virtually any behavior that affects a group or situation. All behavior has an impact and some degree of influence on the surroundings, and every behavior will affect, change, and alter a meeting, discussion, or an organization. Even a small gesture (thumbs up or a dismissive look) to a planned and thoroughly thought-out presentation will affect the person presenting the plan. Though all behavior affects the milieu, the degree of that effect varies.

For example:

- A person who raises a question concerning a topic covered and resolved an hour ago, which the agenda and group have moved on from to other subjects, will derail the current discussion. It will

cause the group to pause, lose momentum, and fall back to something done much earlier.
- An angry outburst will create tension and require different reactions, ones that address emotion and a person, rather than allowing a positive group discussion.
- Nonverbal behavior that communicates impatience, disgust, or scorn will affect the tone and number of contributions from other group members.

All of these behaviors are examples of people negatively affecting the group by asserting some degree of leadership in changing the topic, tone, or participation of the group. The value of these effects may be measured somewhere on the "positive/negative" continuum, depending on other circumstances.

Group dynamics will be in play anytime two or more people come together and begin to interact. It is important for a leader to understand and be aware of the dynamics of any group, especially if that leader is a school administrator working with myriads of groups every day.

Knowing that all behavior can impact (lead) a group allows the leader to be an alert observer to the dynamics of the group, the individual contributions of its members, and how those contributions impact the dynamics and direction. That informed, sensitive, and critical observation provides recognition that the discussion is taking an unintended or nonproductive direction. And recognizing that, the leader can intervene and make adjustments as needed.

Many times, a leader will instinctively note that a discussion or meeting, or even an organization, takes a direction that is unproductive or creates a diversion but doesn't know what to do. To be effective, the leader must have a conscious understanding of what is happening (the group dynamics and the influential leadership) and be able to, and know how to, respond.

Similarly, any member of a group, realizing that everyone and everything affects the meeting or organization, can observe the group dynamics and influential leadership and be more able to follow, understand, adjust, and contribute. That person also realizes that she can not only impact but also influence the direction of the group, assuming some degree of influential leadership.

INFLUENTIAL LEADERSHIP

At one time in the master's degree program for speech at Portland State University in Portland, Oregon, a required text was *The Dynamics of Discussion* (Barnlund and Haiman 1960). Now out of print, this book has a significant and lasting bearing on any understanding, definition, and application of leadership. It provides a different perception of leadership, one that can have a profound effect on the analysis and behavior of a leader, both formal and informal, as a participant in groups.

Dean Barnlund and Franklyn Haiman noted: "This functional approach so aptly named by Irving Knickerbocker in 1948 has been found to be both useful and realistic by research workers in the fields of group leadership and group dynamics" (277–78).

This statement provides an expanded belief and philosophy of leadership. Leadership is any behavior that influences the group or organization. As Barnlund and Haiman stated:

> There is, however, another possible way of viewing leadership. We can think of it as any action that exerts an influence on a group, regardless of its source. With this definition in mind, one sees the "powers behind the throne" to be as much a part of the leadership of the group as the man who happens to hold the gavel. The jokester who breaks up the seriousness of a meeting by provoking outbursts of laughter, or the deviant who delays action on a matter of his disagreement, is also seen as exerting leadership. Even the silent member, by the uncertainty or anxiety he may create in others, or by his contribution to an atmosphere of indifference, has an influence. In short, since every member of the group, if by no other means than his mere presence, has some effect on the discussion, every member is regarded as exerting some degree of leadership.
>
> To view leadership in this way, as the influential *behavior* of all members of a group rather than the authoritative *position* of one, is to see leadership as a more complex and subtle phenomenon than it is often taken to be." (276–77)

PRODUCTIVE LEADERSHIP

Productive leadership is the result of thinking and planning, reacting to conditions and changes, and, when possible, being proactive. Productive leadership also includes outcomes that are positive, ones that make conditions and people better.

All behavior influences groups and processes. Some behavior is positive, some is not. Behavior that is the result of planning and thinking to achieve a desired outcome is more productive than that which is disruptive and obstructive.

In some circumstances, a case can be made for disruptive leadership, such as an unrelated quip to ease tension and break an emotional discussion. Additionally, there are times when a meeting gets bogged down, or the designated leader is incapable of moving the agenda forward. There are also times when a meeting has deteriorated and is off task and becoming unproductive. At those times, it may be appropriate for some kind of disruption to refocus and move in a different direction.

For a leader to be effective and exemplary, her influential behavior should also reflect *productive leadership*, whether in a formal leadership role or as a contributing group member.

Thinking and planning is affected by a combination of static and dynamic behaviors in any group, and not all planning goes as intended. Flexibility and adjustments are often required.

For example, in implementing a strategic plan, one that is developed to realize a desired outcome or vision, adjustments will be required as new information is developed and uncovered. New people will become involved. New information will surface. Results of one phase of the plan will require adjustment to the next phase. In any long-term plan there will be subplans, unexpected reactions, and interruptions that will result in new decisions and directions.

Eventually every plan implementation is reduced down to its individual components. Even a big plan or major response will be defined by a series of smaller individual, collective responses; decisions; and behavior, all of which will affect the outcome.

Here are three examples from the low end of the "influential and productive leadership" continuum to the high end:

- During a meeting, a group member displays nonverbal behavior that communicates disinterest and lack of attention, and then she makes a comment that diverts the group onto an entirely different topic, resulting in an unfinished discussion. (Low end—unproductive)
- During a meeting, an issue is presented. A member of the group considers, analyzes, and thinks about the issue, and then he becomes an oral participant, influencing the discussion and exhibiting behavior that will impact the direction of the discussion or solution. That person and his behavior will influence others and elicit discussion and contributions from them. That person is not the formal leader but contributes in ways that help the group and the leader. (High end—productive)
- A hired executive (principal, superintendent, executive director) has a vision and develops a strategic plan. The plan would include several facets and take place over time. The executive would shepherd the process, outcome, and implementation of the plan. (High end—productive thinking and planning as opposed to calling a meeting with no idea what is needed or where it will go)

BELIEFS AND VALUES

Following is a quote from Dansby Swanson, the top overall pick in the 2015 Major League Baseball draft (as quoted in Quick 2015) that illustrates an important point about effective leadership:

I found that the best leaders are the ones who are servant-based first. There is a difference between leadership and authority. Authority is more of a title, whereas a leader is the one who is always helping someone first. I think that gets lost in translation these days. Just because you have power doesn't make you a leader.

Effective leadership is selfless. Effective leaders do not engage in leadership behavior or activity for the purpose of awards, recognitions, or acclamation. These may come or not. However, they are not *the* motivational factor. The leader may have a natural determination to succeed, or a highly competitive nature, or a deep and internalized commitment to an outcome but does not use them for the purpose of "self." The goal is not to receive recognition or awards. The goal is to work toward realizing the mission; part of the motivation that drives the exemplary leader is "other directed." Others may receive recognition and accolades, but the success of a project or another person is satisfaction enough for the effective leader.

Values play a part, and sometimes the value judgment varies depending on the perspectives of the people involved. Without a doubt, there have been leaders judged either "bad" or "good" throughout history. The most commonly used example is Hitler, who was an effective leader, no doubt. But was he a "good" leader? That is for history to decide, and that judgment is based on the outcomes.

Value statements and beliefs guide *positive leadership*. Examples are:

- Making things better
- Making people successful

Making things better is a rather general statement and can be measured against criteria and values. Things like meeting goals and achieving objective outcomes and targets are examples of ways to measure whether things are better.

There are measurements to judge when or whether things are better — ways to determine whether more students are learning, more parents are satisfied, and teachers are safe and productive. If those measurements say yes, then things are better.

Achieving goals that make other people or conditions better is a value measurement. Examples are:

- Adding healthy menu items
- Painting the faculty lounge area
- Reorganizing teacher teams
- Making a decision about student discipline or homework in a teacher study meeting
- Accepting, declining, or partially implementing a recommendation from research regarding teacher independence and decision making

These and other situations will present themselves to any leader. That leader will make decisions based on her values and whether they make things better.

Making people successful: Educational consultant Larry Lezotte, long-time leader and researcher on effective schooling (http://www.effectiveschools.com), once said that a leader's first obligation is to provide hope. If that is the first obligation, then the second one must be making people successful. A leader must ensure that others experience success, both personally and professionally.

No one wants to fail. People want to be successful. A leader's obligation is to help others experience success. This is accomplished in much the same way that a teacher teaches students:

- Knowing the person's abilities
- Knowing the person's interests
- Assessing the level of achievement and ability
- Applying the knowledge of an individual's abilities, interests, and achievements by putting the person in positions in which she can succeed
- Helping set realistic goals
- Guiding, supporting, and offering feedback to support the achievement of those goals
- Providing the resources to reach those goals

These two statements—*making things better* and *making people successful*—have several other value implications that are also cause for discussion.

Who gets to decide whether things got better? The principal? The superintendent? The school board? The teachers' union? The school or individual teacher? Others? Success to some may not be success to others. For example, the superintendent may want the principal to improve in some way. The principal thinks that things are fine as they are, and everyone in the school agrees. Or the principal may want to change the instructional practices in the school, but the teachers believe that they are successful enough as things are. Administrative and some teacher leaders may recognize school improvements that might be needed that will break traditions and "the way we've always done it."

In the previous examples of who decides, it's usually the person with power that comes from formal authority who makes the decisions.

Does the success of the individual take precedence over the good of the majority? Or vice versa?

- When working to help a teacher improve instructional abilities, at what point does the principal remove the teacher to facilitate teaching and learning in the classroom?
- By mentoring or letting one person carry out a plan to give that person leadership experience, when does the mentor intervene as

the process and outcomes begin to conflict with the thinking of a larger group of teachers?
- Providing leadership experiences and opportunities to one person may affect the morale and cooperation of other teachers, ones who do not like or respect that person, and the overall workings of the school.

Are there times when exceptions are required, and if so, what determines those exceptions?

In a school, for example, some staff members might take the position that things are fine, and everything is working well and nothing needs to get better. People who take that position may resist any change at all. However, nothing is static. What is fine today will be influenced by events and people tomorrow and will require change and adjustment. The issue here becomes taking a stand in the face of resistance and working to continue to make things better—in an ever-changing environment.

When does pushing and working for the success of the other person begin to annoy that person and become counterproductive? And what should be done then? For example, a principal continues to urge a teacher to set other goals, ones that improve instruction, student interactions, or relationships with others. Or the principal continues to suggest an administrative career or a different position in the school, but the teacher resists.

What does an administrator do if helping one person become successful is at the perceived expense of another's goals, ambitions, and success? For example, two people are being mentored or carrying out administrative internships, but there are a limited number of assignments and experiences available in the school or district. One of these two may not have equal responsibilities or opportunities as the other.

A values discussion is entirely appropriate, and an additional significant topic in that discussion is, "Is hurting one or a few to make the many better an acceptable course of action?" The answer to that question is based on values that would be considered in the context of many other related decisions. It becomes a part of the gestalt of decision making.

These are philosophic, and in some cases, practical questions, discussions, and issues. There is certainly the potential for an interesting ethics and value discussion here.

Science is having the information and understanding the goals and concepts. Art is applying that information and realizing outcomes and successes. Effective administrators know how to do that.

Chapter 4
FORMAL AND INFORMAL LEADERSHIP

Formal Leadership

Formal leaders are hired, elected, or promoted to their positions of leadership, and they exist in every organization, profession, or system. The best of these leaders know themselves, realize they have leadership skills, and are aware of their abilities and strengths. Their prior work and success have demonstrated the capacity for deliberate, conscious analysis of planning a course of action or direction and following through to ensure successful completion. Their belief systems, experiences, and skills have been developed from their study and understanding of leadership and people and their progressive, systematic knowledge development, learning experiences, and theoretical study. They also have innate abilities, ones that come naturally.

The Art and Science of Leading relates to an educational model. The following list provides examples of leaders and their constituents, with the desired goals and outcomes of each included in parentheses:

- Teacher to students (student success)
- Department head/team leader to department/team members (student success and teacher success)
- Principal to teachers/staff (school effectiveness and staff success to create and provide elements desirable and required for student success)
- District office administrator to principals (principal success for school, staff, and student success)

Informal Leadership

Leadership also exists at an informal level. Through personality, contribution, and skill, a group member, a teacher, or some other person may be more influential and provide more direction and leadership than the team leader, department head, or administrator does—the formal leader. A committee member may exhibit small or significant influence on the committee process and outcome. This informal leadership may be regular, or it may surface periodically, depending on the expertise and needs of the task and interactions of the participants. Examples include:

- A teacher member of the teaching team may be more skillful in conducting or influencing the team than the designated team leader is.
- A teacher may have background in a topic that is under discussion and one with which no others have familiarity, such as conducting a parent survey and determining the validity of the responses. A

math teacher may have expertise in this area and become the influential, informal leader; an art teacher may not.
- Not all principals, though equal in status, make equal contributions or offer the same quality of ideas and problem solving at principal or administrator meetings. "Leaders of leaders" exist in all leadership groups, and that leadership is a result of both tangibles and intangibles, ones that make that person a leader of leaders.
- In some cases an assigned chairperson may relinquish leadership to a member of the group.
- At times someone other than the designated leader will exert influence and leadership.

This chapter discussed several components of leadership, though perhaps not all. To this point, leadership has been viewed as a many-faceted endeavor, one involving the individualities of people, groups, and the environment, all which affect the others. A Zen proverb states the concept this way: "Nothing ever exists entirely alone. Everything is in relation to everything else" (Gautama Buddha).

GETTING SOMETHING DONE

Productive behavior must be measured against a simple standard: getting something done. It is not enough to plan, or to work with people, or to engage in discussion about a problem or issue. All of these things, and others, are important, but in the final analysis the question must be asked: "Did anything get done?"

- Planning must result in an outcome, in realizing the plan and achieving the goal that the plan was intended to address.
- Working with people must eventually empower them, or help them achieve their goals, or access their expertise.
- Discussing an issue or problem must eventually lead to some conclusions, or follow-up plan, or some action to address the issue or plan.

Although all behavior can influence—*lead*—a group, at some point on the continuum that behavior should move to *productive leadership*, and something should get done. When does behavior that influences—leads—become productive and contribute toward getting things accomplished? The following chapter discusses the beliefs and values that measure the transition toward productive leadership.

FIVE

Effective, Exemplary Leaders

Exemplary: Deserving of imitation; commendable (*Webster's*).

In her book, *Quiet: The Power of Introverts in a World That Can't Stop Talking*, Susan Cain (2013) wrote:

> Our lives are shaped as profoundly by personality as by gender or race. And the single most important aspect of personality . . . is where we fall on the introvert-extrovert spectrum. Our place on this continuum influences our choice of friends and mates, and how we make conversation, resolve differences, and show love. It affects the careers we choose and whether or not we succeed at them. . . . It governs how likely we are to exercise, commit adultery, function well without sleep, learn from our mistakes, place big bets . . . , delay gratification, be a good leader, and ask "what if?" (3)

What is it that makes some leaders more effective—better—than others? The personality traits with which they are born, ones that affect how they think, interact, and much more, are a deciding factor in identifying, predicting, and recognizing the most effective leaders; these traits significantly contribute to the art of leadership.

Following are examples of ineffective leaders based on personality traits:

- A high school administrator hired a band director. The band director was a master musician and had excellent student rapport, and the band's sound improved, as did individual students as musicians. However, the director overran the music budget and did not submit it in a timely way during the budgeting process. He also did not properly monitor or inventory equipment. As a result, significant needs in the music department were not considered or brought to the attention of his administrator. Music equipment and instru-

ments disappeared, and the school's investment in those was lost. Scheduled events went unattended, buses were not ordered, and registration materials went unsent.
- This wonderful musician had no organizational skills. Nothing the administrator attempted could teach those skills. He just didn't think that way. He wasn't born with that aptitude.
- A consultant who was working with a middle school to assess student learning, teacher effectiveness, and programs consistent with the age of young adolescents had frequent interaction with the principal. This principal held a degree, a license, had excellent grades in high school and university coursework, and generally did a good job of meeting deadlines, responding to others, and keeping the school safe and orderly. However, in every meeting the consultant attended, the principal's verbal contributions were off topic and demonstrated a lack of *tracking the discussion*, let alone leading it.

  This principal was missing key analytic listening and topic relationship abilities and group processing skills. Some degree of analytic ability and tracking discussion can be taught. However, instincts cannot be taught. If analysis and processing skills have to be taught, they will be formal and stilted. They may not be applied appropriately and will not be instinctive. The person will not excel at them.
- Association board members and the president were elected after campaigning. The elections to office were usually based on relationships with other members, reputation, and regions of the country. Very seldom were background, experience, or skills factors in these elections. As a result, some of the popularly elected presidents lacked basic communication ability or effective leadership skills.

In some cases, the officers, though they were wonderful people and successful in their own schools and careers, were confronted with situations for which they were unprepared. They were conscientious and mission driven, but they needed support from others who had confronted similar challenges and circumstances. Some of those officers recognized the need for assistance and support. There may be others who don't recognize they need assistance and support, but should have.

How does a leader develop a repertoire of skills, abilities, and experiences that result in successful and effective leadership?

CHANGE

Change is a given. It is a constant, and the list of changes is long and ample. Medicine. Fashion trends. Educational research. Technology. Travel. Population and age demographics. Virtually everything.

People change too, within parameters.

Things Change

Life, and everything connected to it, is fluid and constantly changing, and it takes little observation to see evidence of change. If there is one clear and predictable characteristic about today's world, it is that "things change." It is the one inevitability. A leader must recognize, accept, and think in terms of change. What *is* today will *not be* tomorrow. People will be different; they will feel emotionally or think intellectually different about things one day to the next. Conditions will change; new information will surface resulting in a need to change the plan. People will grow or digress. Funding will increase or decrease. Everything will change to some degree, either imperceptibly or to such a significant degree that it impacts planning in a major way.

A candidate for a principal position was one of three finalists but did not get the job. She asked a trusted friend and administrator what she might have done wrong. Actually, she did nothing wrong, and that is what her administrator told her:

> You were a finalist, and that makes you successful. Your application was good, your references were supportive, and there were no negatives attached to your applications. After being named a finalist, it was out of your control. At that point, it is a matter of *fit*, to the district and those interviewing and hiring. One of the interview committee members may have been having a bad day and was ready to not like anyone who was interviewed. The next day, she may have been having a good day, her filter would have been different, she may have been more receptive to people and your responses, and things would have been different. Circumstances in the district or school may have been such that your leadership style didn't match. Next year, those issues of today may be resolved, and you would match more closely.

The administrator continued, "The point is, things change. And when things change, the match changes."

An effective leader will understand that change is inevitable and be aware of how things are evolving. She will anticipate changes, thinking ahead in terms of what to do next or differently, as she sees what is coming. It is easy to be comfortable with the status quo and prefer to think "Things are good, so why change?" That is comfortable, but it just doesn't work.

One of the tenets of effective schooling is that if you are not an improving school, you are a school in decline. Staying the same is impossible and is not an option. Everything is changing around you and, in the process, changing you and your organization. A leader can either recognize, influence, and control the organization changes, or just let them happen by default. Simply put, the people and organization have to adjust with the changes in the environment. It is the leader's responsibility to guide the concept of a plan, see change, and adjust.

Here is an example.

Inherent in the Effective School's improvement philosophy (http://www.effectiveschools.com) is that a school cannot remain static. People, conditions, and elements are changing all around it, and if the school does not continue to be aware of those changes and adjust to them, that school will fall behind and thus be in a state of decline.

A conversation that a principal was having with a staff member illustrates the point on a personal, classroom level. Wondering why she was having such a difficult year, the staff member said, "I'm doing the same thing I've done for twenty years, and things that have worked." The principal responded this way:

> The children are different from those you worked with over the years. Things have gradually been changing in student attitudes and interests, in their culture, lifestyles, and the world around them. The families from which they come are different. The demographics of the community are different. Inventions, toys, tools, and progress have changed uses of free time, attention spans, transportation, and other elements of the school and student lives. You cannot apply methods and information that was valid twenty years ago to today's students. New planning, new instructional research on brain development, learning styles, and an awareness of societal changes must be factored into your planning [it should be noted that the staff member was not appreciative].

In the sense that a leader recognizes change, adjusts to and plans for it, and supports others as they do the same, every effective leader is a change agent. Style may define the *how* of being a change agent, but the common thread is that things change and people must recognize and adjust to change.

Do People Change? Not So Much

As Simon and Garfunkel aptly put it in "The Boxer" (1968): "after changes, we are more or less the same."

Not too long ago on the *Late Show with David Letterman*, Donald Trump, a presidential candidate, was a guest. He is a personality in his own right: very wealthy and a huge success in commercial development. Letterman was asking Trump about his childhood and teenage years, talking about some of his youthful behavior and independence, rebelliousness, and interactions with others as he was growing up. The host asked, "Are you still like that?" The guest smiled and said, "Yes." He went on to say, "You are born a certain way, and it doesn't really change that much. I think you are born one way and you stay that way the rest of your life" (Letterman 2013).

The essence of this section is that a person can be taught leadership concepts, functions, and skills (the science). However, unless that person is born with certain aptitudes, he will have a difficult, if not impossible, time mastering and applying them (the art) and will not become an exemplary leader. Examples of science versus art follow:

- A person can be given the tools for organization, but if she doesn't have the capacity or aptitude to use those tools, organization will not come naturally.
- A person can be taught that "everything affects everything" or "cause and effect," but if he does not have a natural aptitude to make connections, he will have a difficult time seeing how things affect each other.
- A person can be taught the scientific method, but if she does not have a natural curiosity or an aptitude for problem solving or the ability to apply a concept to a variety of situations, she will have a difficult time applying the method to real-life issues.

In an earlier reference from *Quiet* (Cain 2013):

> Our lives are shaped as profoundly by personality as by gender or race. And the single most important aspect of personality . . . is where we fall on the introvert-extrovert spectrum. Our place on this continuum influences our choice of friends and mates, and how we make conversation, resolve differences, and show love. It affects the careers we choose and whether or not we succeed at them. . . . It governs how likely we are to exercise, commit adultery, function well without sleep, learn from our mistakes, place big bets . . . , delay gratification, be a good leader, and ask "what if?" (3)

Cain cited many research studies and psychology expert references supporting the notion that nature determines much of who we are and how we act throughout our lives. Nature provides the base. Nurture plays a part in how that base is developed and into what kinds of behavior, values, and leadership our innate abilities evolve.

Certainly, and hopefully, as people age they develop and become more skilled. They mature; their brains grow and change and process information differently. Decision making is developed. Inevitably, they amass a breadth of knowledge and experiences. The nurturing they experience, the environment in which they are raised, the values to which they are subjected all impact how they and everyone else develops and grows. Additionally, everyone is born with innate tendencies and personality proclivities, and while people will develop in their behaviors and personalities, the basic pattern is established when they are born. In modern terms, it is in their DNA.

DNA doesn't change—neither does a person change in ways contrary to their DNA. Sometimes training and development will alter basic tendencies, and experience and nurturing will affect how their innate abilities are manifested. Behavior is affected by innate abilities, and though there are exceptions to every rule, the research is sophisticated and clear. Consider these examples:

- An organized person does not become overly random.
- An impulsive person who has a pattern of responding emotionally and without thinking may have difficulty developing a consistent pattern of thought before acting.
- A pessimistic person does not evolve into an optimist or vice versa.
- Authoritative, controlling people have difficulty with shared decision making.
- An esoteric thinker, or a random thought processor, has trouble with concrete, sequential thinking.

Pick any example. There are many. Training, learning, development, nurture, and practice can alter innate tendencies and behavior. However, by definition, innate tendencies do not change, are never far from the surface, and influence behavior, including leadership behavior. Tendencies may be masked or compensated for but they do not change. In this sense, people do not change. Who a person is in grade school is basically who he will be in high school and into adulthood.

If an administrator has had experience at all levels of schooling and worked with adults in many settings, she, as an insightful educator, will be able to observe a student and predict with a high degree of success how that student will look and behave as an adult. That same insightful educator can observe students in the middle school level and, particularly if they have spent time in a high school, can look at those young adolescents and predict how they will look and develop as a high school student. Conversely, in working with adults, it is sometimes interesting to look back and imagine them as they progressed through middle school, high school, university, and young adulthood.

Other skills (communication, ambiguity tolerance, objectivity, power, courage, organization) and the appropriate, ethical use of power are further considerations, ones that are necessary when considering the exemplary leader and will be discussed in coming chapters.

FORMAL PREPARATION

A reasonably intelligent and motivated person can learn the science of administrative leadership skills. Knowing the science is critical, and effective administrative leaders must have that background and knowledge. As part of that preparation, coursework and reading are necessary for several reasons:

- Exposure to the issues and requirements of administration and leadership helps leaders meet the expectations around them in any administrative position they may hold.
- Structured theories of administration, leadership, and foundational knowledge help leaders make sense out of their personal experiences, tendencies, reactions, and behaviors and allow them to think through answers to questions like "What if . . . " and "If this happens . . ." That knowledge helps define and structure what might otherwise be vague inclinations and places them into leadership situations and contexts.
- The pedagogy of teaching and learning must be learned. There are several issues and topics that must be mastered (e.g., student learning theory and research, differentiated planning, young adolescent development, standards) as well as other administrative requirements such as school structures, budgeting, instructional leadership, research, school improvement, staff supervision, and contract management.

Coursework can address all of these and more, but it contributes only one aspect of formal, active leadership preparation.

MENTORS

It is unusual to find a successful administrator or leader who could not list one or more mentors who made a difference in their background, training, and belief system—and their success. Mentors provide opportunities and guidance. A mentor is a person who can be counted on for support, training, and advice and used as a sounding board. To be effective, every potential educational administrator/leader will have to have administrative experiences. Those are usually provided by a mentor and accessed as part of a current assignment or as a practicum. There is additional information on mentors and mentoring in chapter 16, Future Leaders.

NATURAL OR INNATE ABILITY

Preparation (including mentoring) helps an administrator/leader reach a B-level. However, to reach the level of an exemplary leader, an A+, certain natural abilities must be in place. Those attributes can't be taught. Either they are in place inherently and naturally, or they are not. In this sense, the exemplary leader is born, not developed. They are the ones who significantly contribute to the art of administrative leadership.

Following are examples of natural or innate abilities that, if developed, are reflected in exemplary leadership:

- Instincts—know and trust them and have a track record of good instincts, ones that were proven right when action was based on them
- Organization, including the ability to prioritize
- A sense of mission, one that is internalized, overriding, and selfless
- Intelligence
- Analytic thinking

Other specific characteristics of exemplary leaders can be found in assessment instruments. Many instruments describe and offer tools to assess leadership characteristics (Internet search: educational administrative assessment instruments). Two particularly useful ones include:

- The most recent document provided by the Council of Chief State School Officials (CCSSO)—*Educational Leadership Policy Standards*. Based on research and study, this document describes six standards necessary to successful school leadership. The document is being used for preparation, professional growth, and assessment.
- The National Association of Secondary School Principal's (NASSP) Administrator Assessment, a program that engages potential administrators in a multiday series of exercises intended to identify administrative and leadership skills. According to Dick Flanary, former deputy executive director of programs and services, "[T]he purpose of the NASSP Assessment Center [see appendix 2] is twofold: First, the assessment center accurately diagnoses the presence and strength of skills to assist in selection and development. Second, the center forms skill awareness for effective practice and serves as a baseline diagnosis for individual development" (personal communication, April 21, 2014).

Two other useful resources for identifying leadership attributes are Gallup/Selection Research, Inc.'s (1979) perceiver characteristics and effective schools research. Additionally, there are many psychological, personality, and organizational development tools and materials that provide self-assessments (Internet search: personality inventories).

Regardless of how leadership characteristics and innate abilities are measured or identified, it is possible to prepare a *good* administrator, one who will be effective. However, without certain inborn potential for specific skills and attributes, that person will not reach the *exemplary* level.

Two other factors, experience and the knowledge that comes with it, are critical to success, though the degree of each varies depending on the position in the hierarchical structure, the complexity of the milieu, and the level of elected office.

EXPERIENCE ENHANCES FUTURE PERFORMANCE

Some examples:

A high school teacher will have one set of experiences, challenges, and coping abilities as she begins her career. That same person will later have more confidence and ability and will be more of a leader and expert in the areas of education. Every year adds to the foundation of experiences that provide context and confidence later on.

However, a teacher will not have been afforded the same experiences or knowledge base as a person who has served as a principal. As a result, a teacher is not normally moved directly from the classroom to the district office without having experienced the principalship.

This is not to say that people with less experience and background should *not* be in a particular leadership position. Appointment to an administrative position depends on many factors, and some of them are not related to preparation, competence, and leadership abilities. Some of those factors are:

- How deep and experienced is the candidate pool?
- Whom do you know? Who owes whom political favors? Who has favorites?
- Who are the favorites?
- For an elected office, who makes up the electorate?

It is unlikely that any one person has *all* the desired and required skills and abilities for leadership to support all the others in an organization. Sometimes it takes more than one person to provide resources and knowledge. A complementary team has a better chance of doing so. Leadership is obtained through securing advisers, engaging in continual professional development, and self-reflection. And leaders with limited experience who find themselves in administrative positions too early can maximize their leadership of a school or organization by forming a team, one that includes individuals with complementary skills and abilities.

The wise leader is one who possesses self-awareness and works with other people—people who bring to the organization diverse opinions and perspectives and a variety of abilities. To be an *exemplary leader*, one must also have certain innate abilities as well as experience, training, background, and coursework/reading. With that combination, the exemplary leader has a higher probability for successful leadership and realizing the mission.

SIX
Instructional Leadership

The Christian Science Monitor and *The Hechinger Report* followed Krystal Hardy, a principal, through her inaugural year at Sylvanie Williams College Prep elementary charter school in New Orleans (Tyre 2015):

> Being a school principal has never been easy, of course. Traditionally the role was like being the chief executive officer and face of the school . . . hired teachers, interpreted directives from the district and state, and balanced the budget. Day to day this meant wrestling with innumerable smaller tasks: handling the concerns of parents, disciplining unruly kids, negotiating food service contracts, and figuring out what to do with the bulky air conditioner in the gym.
>
> The new generation of principals . . . especially those who work in urban schools, has become far more involved with what happens in the classroom. Spurred by new state laws that call for improved methods of teacher evaluation, many districts across the country are looking for principals to serve as instructional leaders . . . ones who will help teachers improve, rewarding those deemed "most effective" and firing those who aren't.

An intellectual mastery of teaching and learning theory will contribute to a command of the science in administrative instructional leadership. Effectively working with teachers and principals and others in the system to maximize student success and learning—that is the art.

The literature regarding instructional leadership is voluminous. Thomas Hoerr (2007) offered an accepted definition of instructional leadership: "[The principal] needs to be the educational visionary, offering direction and expertise to ensure that students learn" (84). In essence, instructional leadership is the action that a principal takes or delegates to others to promote growth in student learning.

Articles, book seminars, research papers, and courses address the leader's roles and responsibilities in teaching and learning. This chapter will highlight the critical behaviors attributed to instructional leadership. The base for these ideas is the assumption that the *exemplary* leader in the field of education *is* an instructional leader—one who possesses a solid scientific foundation knowledge base about instructional leadership and effectively applies that foundation to the daily activities in a school or district, both a scientist and an artist.

Although the specific definition and earlier reference is to the principal, it can and should be expanded to all leaders in the organization.

There was a principal who asked himself at the beginning of every day, "What can I do today that will contribute to instructional leadership?" Following are a few of the ways he answered that question and demonstrated instructional leadership:

- Helping a teacher identify professional growth opportunities
- Sitting in on a class lesson and providing feedback
- Conducting a meeting that was focused on school improvement
- Participating in or observing an all-school interdisciplinary team meeting
- Helping a student understand how to be tolerant of another student who was less gifted
- Walking through the school and complimenting teachers and students on teaching/learning/relationships
- Giving specific, positive feedback as an affirmation to a teacher who yesterday was questioning her effectiveness
- Writing an exhaustive, end-of-the-year teacher evaluation, one that included a review of the year, affirmation of good work, progress toward the year's goals, suggestions for next year, a reflection on information gathered through formal and informal classroom visits, progress toward goals, and general concerns and goals for the coming year. This exhaustive summary is not only helpful; it also acknowledges and affirms the teacher and demonstrates to the teacher that the principal/leader cares enough to take the time to gather the information and complete the lengthy evaluation. It reflects and demonstrates a grasp of the science of teaching and leadership. It also, by engaging in this kind of personal interest and thorough evaluation, reflects the art of leadership.

Every day, this principal tried to include activities that reflected instructional leadership. Later, as a district office administrator, he did the same with principals he supervised. He engaged in many other conscious instructional leadership activities with other district and school personnel as he worked with district programs, such as promoting technology in schools and classrooms. He worked with principals and district committees composed of district building staff members.

These are all conscious examples of educational leadership, by being an "educational visionary, offering direction and expertise to ensure that students learn" (Hoerr 2007, 84). Any instructional leader could create an individual list, but the important element is that she do it consciously and purposefully. After a while it becomes instinctive, and instructional leadership activities are included in the daily routine.

Each school or district that states as its goal "student success," or includes student success in its mission, must have educational leaders. Every leader of each one of these institutions must believe in herself an instructional leader and activate that belief through appropriate action.

LEADERS HAVE A VISION

If a leader doesn't have a vision, she should get one. If a person doesn't know where she is going, how can she develop a plan to get there? Or know when she is there? Without a vision for the future, what are the reasons people and organizations do what they are doing?

Successful leaders have in mind a picture of how the organization should look, what it should be doing, how it is realizing its mission and goals—tomorrow, next year, and beyond. Without knowing what should be happening and how things should work and look, it would be impossible to consciously plan a successful, outcome-driven course of action.

"[Krystal] Hardy's job centered more on academic progress, which demanded both a broad vision and pointillist attention to detail. She had to provide teachers . . . with a general blueprint for educational achievement as well as specific guidance to improve their instructions" (Tyre 2015).

Following are examples of vision at several levels of education. Inherent in these examples is the understanding that things change, and as such, planning is affected by many influences, making the plan dynamic. Planning requires constant monitoring, assessment, and adaptation as the leader keeps the vision in mind:

- A teacher has a vision about how his classroom should look and work—what should be happening in the classroom to ensure and facilitate the success of every student.
- A teacher leader has a vision not only for the classroom but also for the school. That leader works with others to realize the school vision and both understands and supports the plan to work toward it.
- A principal has a clear, conceptual, and practical three- to five-year vision for how a school should operate and teachers and classrooms should maximize learning; that principal monitors the activities of the school as it works toward realizing the vision.
- A district administrator should have in mind a clear three- to five-year vision, an idea of what principals should be doing, how

schools should be processing and improving, and what activities and growth goals should be in place to realize student success.
- An association director should have a clear idea of what the association must do to realize its mission and know how it looks and operates three to five years in the future. Among other things, she should have a clear picture of membership, services, attitude, the "fabric" of the association, what process activities should be taking place, the relationship with the board and officers, and the level of impact and significance the association carries with other organizations and entities.

The effective leader will have a clear vision. It isn't enough that only the leader or administrator has the vision. The vision must be shared and prominent in all aspects of the organization in all communications. The administrative leader will describe and share the vision and work with others in the organization to realize that vision. In that sense, the leader must spend time constantly clarifying and communicating the vision. He is continually working at "selling" the vision to gain buy-in from all constituents in the organization. Benchmarks should be established, measured, and celebrated. As things change, so should the plan to realize the vision. Vision is critical for any leader in any organization.

REALIZING THE VISION

A leader must move beyond simply a vision, or an idea, or a set of goals. The leader must have in place a strategic plan, a set of incremental activities, events, or behaviors that move the organization toward realization of the vision.

WORKING WITH PEOPLE IS INHERENT IN LEADERSHIP

"I believe that if we are going to move forward, it is . . . because we are a team" (Tyre 2015). Working with people is a key element for a leader to realize the vision and is an element of instructional leadership at all levels. The principal cannot do it all. Schools are a collection of professionals and other stakeholders who have more direct contact with students; some have additional or complementary expertise, and others have a wider range of influence than the single person who is the principal. To realize the vision, everyone must be engaged.

Research supports the contention that school outcomes and student learning are influenced by distributive leadership (working with other people). Distributive leadership is based on the assumption that tasks are spread over a group of people in a school. Those people are teachers, parents, and district staff—people who are included to improve student achievement (Canole and Young 2013, 23). More specifically:

- Teachers have a responsibility to their students. Teachers who are instructional leaders are also involved in school improvement and members of teams that function effectively, and they assume other professional responsibilities.
- Teachers who are instructional leaders will share ideas, mentor new staff members, and work with teachers and administrators in school policy, environment, and student success school-wide.
- The principal, as an instructional leader, must have a working knowledge of group processes, facilitate curriculum study and work groups, and be involved with groups that plan curriculum that include teacher leaders. The principal must be able to assist as others align curriculum to standards and as they analyze and address student data. However, the principal does not need to have an intimate working knowledge of every curricular subject.
- The principal, as an instructional leader, must be able to assist teachers with goal setting and help them reach those goals. The principal must know and be able to help teachers in the elements of lesson planning, student/teacher relationships, and the science of teaching. The principal must know how to use this knowledge and to observe and help teachers be more effective by using it herself. The principal does not need to have an intimate knowledge of every curricular subject to be helpful to teachers, but the principal does have to understand the science of effective instruction.
- The principal, as an instructional leader working with others, helping them be successful, and realizing their goals, must be present in classrooms watching teachers teach and students learn. Knowing how and what a teacher is doing allows the principal to build on the teacher's strengths and systematically focus on areas for refinement, or even improvement. By being present in the classrooms the principal obtains critical knowledge that contributes to her instructional leadership, knowledge about the strengths and needs for growth of both students and teachers, and the tone of the school. It does something more, something significant that is the art of leadership. It demonstrates to the teacher that the principal cares enough to help and to know what is happening in the classroom and, importantly, cares about the teacher as a person and professional.
- The principal, as an instructional leader, must be able to analyze data and facilitate the process of goal setting. The principal must be able to facilitate a school improvement plan and know how to access the resources necessary to meet improvement goals. However,

the principal does not have to be a curriculum expert in all possible goal areas for school improvement.
- The superintendent, as an instructional leader, must put priority on student learning and curriculum alignment, know how students are progressing in all the schools, and work with the principals to ensure school improvement processes. The superintendent does not necessarily have to know the skills and strengths of all the people in all the schools.
- The superintendent is accountable to the board. The superintendent as instructional leader keeps the board informed on curriculum issues, professional development, student progress, and school improvement. The superintendent as instructional leader involves the board on committees, projects, and district goal development.
- The executive director hires and supervises staff. The executive director as instructional leader works closely with staff members to assess their abilities and dreams, helps them set realistic goals, and supports them with resources and opportunities to realize those goals.
- The association executive director is responsible to the association's board, members, and volunteers. The executive director as instructional leader will help the board do its work by providing structure, ideas, and resources for the members and volunteers to be involved and participating in the mission and product development of the organization.

ALL THE TIME

Not even an exemplary instructional leader embraces all the elements or characteristics of leadership even though that element or characteristic may be important to others and should be considered. The exemplary leader may not embrace some elements, but she does them anyway. Take icebreakers, for example.

Sometimes there is value in using icebreaking activities. They can relieve discomfort or stress, help meeting participants know each other, and get them talking to one another in a relaxed, informal, and nonthreatening atmosphere. Some people enjoy them and, when working with people, the leader should recognize and accept icebreakers.

It does not necessarily follow that by recognizing the value of icebreaking activities the leader enjoys or conducts them well. Some leaders may actually dislike icebreakers, particularly when people employ them inappropriately by making them too long, too silly, or too numerous. Nonetheless, a leader must recognize that some people like icebreakers and are good at them, and they should be incorporated when they set the stage for what follows. A leader must recognize the interests and desires of others and include in her leadership style behaviors that she may otherwise choose not to do. Icebreakers are one example.

Another example is reflected by this paraphrased comment from a successful high school principal who said he sat for hours in his office talking with a particular person: "He was the union president and he'd drop by late in the afternoon, usually just as I was getting ready to go home. He was single, had nowhere to go, and would want to sit and just visit. I didn't approve of his position in the union, his sense of self-importance, or the way he conducted the work of the association. I didn't necessarily want to be friends, but it was important for the organization and for my relationship with the staff and the union, and I sat there and had hours of friendly conversation."

Management is critical to move an organization toward a vision, but the teacher, the principal, and the superintendent (the administrative leaders) must do more than manage. If the vision is to make people successful and to ensure that students learn, they must be instructional leaders.

WORKING WITH A VARIETY OF PROCESSES

Schools are a complex aggregate of people and activity. Leadership of schools is also complex. It is a proposition that requires planning and orderly procedures to guide the aggregate toward student achievement while providing a safe and orderly environment (safe and orderly is addressed in chapter 8, Management). Thus, the instructional leader must be versed in several processes:

- Monitoring staff and student data and progress, staff development and goal setting, and effective school structures that support instruction
- Knowledge of instructional practice, teaching, and learning pedagogy
- Group dynamics
- Data gathering and analysis and how to apply it to school and organizational improvement processes
- Effective supervision and evaluation of staff—beyond the legal requirements and the hiring and firing authority
- Curriculum development and alignment
- Involving stakeholders who are affected by decisions

PREPARATION

Just as the effective teacher must be prepared, so too must the instructional leader be prepared. Although it is necessary to reach the highest level of leadership, it is not enough to rely on natural ability and instincts alone. Formal study, preparation through reading and discussion, experiences (the wider and more diverse, the better), disappointments and successes—all of these and more contribute to the preparation of exemplary leaders, especially instructional leaders. Instructional leaders know, understand, and have process skills in:

- Curriculum development
- Staff supervision
- Organizational development
- Communication skills
- School improvement processes
- Learning theory
- Human development

Preparation comes from schooling, study, observing others, and experience. The science, formal learning, and an experiential background in knowing how and when to employ a certain process will contribute to the confidence, credibility, and expertise that any instructional leader will bring to the position and the organization. Without this preparation, the repertoire and range of options from which to draw will limit his credibility and artistic ability to appropriately lead by responding to issues and situations.

SEVEN

The Age of Standards

Implications for Effective Leadership

Gary Sehorn

A BIGGER STAGE

Everything changes, and since change is a given in education, effective leaders recognize and adapt to shifting contexts, including national standards, which are a part of the leadership gestalt.

The recent ascendency of standards provides challenges and opportunities that tap both the art and the science of leadership. Essentially, what has happened is that building-level administrators are now doing their work on a bigger stage with new actors and forces beyond the traditional circles. School leaders must be skillfully and artfully engaged with these actors and forces to practice effective leadership.

THE SHIFTING LOCUS OF CONTROL

Before the triumph of national standards and the testing and accountability systems that mushroomed in their wake, local schools were at the center of the thinking concerning school excellence. The term "site based" was preeminent, and the expectation was that each school could do great things for students based on local decisions about what best suited the students and the community.

There were policy and resource parameters, but the locus of control was the school, and in the middle of that work was the principal. Significant mandates from beyond the school were rare, and district leadership could often either ignore or give short shrift to such expectations. That allowed school administrators to maintain a robust view of the whole child and, in working with teachers and support staff, the whole person.

That has changed and for good reason. There were thin spots and gaps in the site-based world. Groups of students—especially minority and low-income students—were not successful, and those failures were often hidden in large, well-regarded, middle-class schools. High expectations were not held for all students, and there were inequities of opportunity everywhere.

Programs such as Effective Schooling and other school improvement processes were unsuccessful in assisting administrators, schools, teachers, and stakeholders in many communities to address those inequities; those pervasive problems helped fuel the standards and accountability movement. The noble root of this recent reform effort is a mission to address these very concerns. Governmental action at the state and federal levels targeted at this work has been joined by powerful advocacy organizations. The challenge for school leaders is to deftly work with this expanded circle of power outside the school so the systemic focus can remain at the local level.

ADMINISTRATORS AS TRANSLATORS AND INTERPRETERS

Effective leaders in the current context leverage the expanded external mandates, expectations, and resources to support meaningful and sustainable change. Administrators have always had to translate, prioritize, and interpret. The difference today is that this work must now include messages, mandates, and expectations from more sources and with much more specificity and accountability, so this work has increased in complexity.

Successful small-district superintendents routinely provide this kind of filtering, sorting, and framing, in part because they don't have layers of specialized program leaders with whom to share the work. Effective principals have always done this too, especially in larger districts. Principals serve as "gatekeepers" and "translators" of mandates and initiatives of various stripes that come from the district office and elsewhere. Enhancing and sharpening this skill is now of particular importance for school leadership.

Sometimes this means saying no on behalf of the school, even when a yes would please the powers above and the powers beyond the district. Administrators routinely say no in ways that are often unnoticed but that are essential for schools to operate. Anyone taking the time to catalog all the state statutes and regulations that apply to the operation of schools, plus all that district policy requires, and piling on the stacks of expectations from district programs and initiatives would clearly see that principals simply cannot lead "by the book" and merely focus on "fidelity" of implementation.

FIDELITY AND SCHOOL MISSION

The new actors who have inserted themselves into the work of school improvement often enter the school in the form of grants. Just like federal and state grant programs, these dollars come with specific expectations to be followed with fidelity to assure local educators don't stray from the approved script. In many cases, the fidelity demanded is complete obedience, and school administrators are expected to assume the role of compliance officer.

At times, the political reality is that a school must go along with an outside set of expectations. In those cases, the wise leader works to adapt the new requirement as much as possible and minimize the negative effect.

For example, consider a situation whereby a new grant opportunity from a private foundation comes to a principal's desk. District leadership strongly encourages schools to apply. Wise leaders consider the specific programmatic elements of the grant to determine whether it is aligned to the core mission of the school. The essential question is: "Does this resource help us achieve our goals?" Then come the artful questions about the politics of the expectation, the timelines, and the match between the grant's demands and the school staff. The essential questions here: "Are we in a position to say no? Are we equipped to fold this grant into our work without disruption?"

SCHOOLING AS A MARKETPLACE

The standards and accountability era has also approached students and parents as customers in a large marketplace of schooling where choice is envisioned as the fairy dust that will help children soar to success. Provisions for school choice are often woven into the fabric of grant funding and educational policies. Directed by mandates on how to improve and prodded by a marketplace competition, local schools are expected to rouse from complacency and dramatically improve learning for students.

Central to this market view of education is popular opinion concerning individual schools, just as customers rate local restaurants. Schools have always sought to maintain a positive image in the community, but the reality of school choice in various forms puts added expectations on the principal to actively manage and advertise a positive image.

Typically schools are in the media when test scores are reported, and school-to-school comparisons are the focus. This implies that the "better" schools can be determined by those test scores. However, the mission and motivation of most educators is rooted in a much broader definition of success for children. Most teachers appreciate that students come to school with unique intellectual, creative, social, emotional, physical, and spiritual needs and aspirations that are all aspects of "success" and cannot be compartmentalized or reduced to test scores. *That gestalt is at the core of teaching, and it anchors the school's moral mission.* It offers the light by which school administrators must lead, wisely recognizing the reality of test scores, school marketing, and comparisons, but maintaining professional space for teachers.

DEFINING SUCCESS

To achieve this, school administrators have to develop and maintain a robust definition of student success that reflects the school's moral mission. While not ignoring the public reporting of test scores and school comparisons, local schools must craft more demanding and comprehensive accountability indicators that honor the whole child, tap into community values, and rally local stakeholders.

Rather than looking to federal directives, state policy, or powerful national foundations, school leadership must recenter on the local community, which can be a deep well of support for the school.

This significant challenge calls for principals to engage with their local school communities in dynamic ways. Top-down changes typically bypass the local community, especially when that community is poor and majority-minority.

In many locations, the chasm between communities and their local schools has widened as the standards and accountability movement has grown. However, local communities have the most riding on the success of their children, and even distressed neighborhoods are storehouses of assets to be identified, valued, and braided into the mission and programming of the local school.

A deep irony is confirmed annually by the Gallup-Kappan survey: the closer parents and community members are to their local school, the better they like it; the further away, the more media messages and pervasive narratives of failure and danger take over. This accounts for Americans' support of national and state policy efforts to "fix" terrible, failing schools *out there*, meanwhile worrying that *their* local schools are being distracted or damaged by all those meddling outsiders and excessive testing.

COMMUNITIES AS FULL PARTNERS

The rich engagement with the local community advocated here also assumes a different approach to vision. One of the essential qualities of a successful leader has been the ability to cast a vision and engage others in the pursuit of that vision. In the site-based era, vision work was local and, especially at the elementary and middle levels, generally took into account the whole child. In the standards and accountability era, vision has often become a muddled concept featuring an external locus of control and subservience to the national test score obsession.

In the current context, it is the duty of the principal to foster the development of the school as a powerful, moral, *whole* community, create space for teachers and staff to be the professionals they are called to be, and simultaneously honor parents and patrons as full partners in service to the *whole* child. Administrators must lead an ongoing conversation with local communities using their leadership skills, knowledge, and strategies. That conversation must feature humble listening that uncovers local assets and aspirations and fosters robust collaboration. That conversation provides a process to define and refine a local consensus understanding of "success."

Such a definition must account for external mandates, but it will be grounded in the local community. Even so, it is the principal's moral duty throughout the conversation to assure that the inequities that lurk at the door seeking advantage for some at the expense of others are confronted boldly. Commitment to the common good is always the responsibility of the school leader.

Deep, ongoing community partnerships as described here may not lead to a spiffy vision-based banner hanging in the school entryway, but it will yield a living, powerful, commonly held moral mission. Such a vision has tremendous power to guide collaborative work that is understood by all to be the joint responsibility of the community and its school.

CREATING SPACE FOR THE ART AND SCIENCE OF SCHOOL LEADERSHIP

This approach requires leadership that is skilled in occasionally tacking against the prevailing winds, using the energy of current realities rather than fighting them directly, to maintain the space to do the collaboration, learning, and growing at the heart of principals' work as instructional leaders.

Thomas Sergiovanni used the term "building in canvas" to describe the leadership practice of presenting a public institutional face to district leadership and the larger community that meets the legitimate expectations of those beyond the school walls. The phrase is a reference to a strategy employed by the Allies in World War II. Using wood and canvas, mock planes and tanks gave the Germans an inflated impression of Allied strength.

In schools, the goal is to comply with the legitimate needs of the governing authority while making room for the school community to keep focused on the core mission. Often, this is all about translation. How does a leader help the organization receive an external mandate that cannot be ignored and recast it, with integrity, as an aspect of the local school's mission and vision?

Leadership is a gestalt that is both art and science. Standards, testing, and the accountability systems so prominent in the media today are part of the science of leadership. So are influential nongovernmental change agents. Understanding the interconnections among all these forces and applying essential leadership skills and knowledge to reestablish the local school as the locus of control is part of the art of leadership, and it is here that all the ingredients of leadership (as described in other chapters in this book) are required and in evidence: the intuitive and the formal preparation and experience. This interconnection should be included as part of the vision (chapter 6, Instructional Leadership) and the strategic plan (chapter 13, Goals: Planning, Organizational, Individual).

Administrators who fail to intentionally lead at the boundary where the local school and the wider world meet will struggle to lead in the school, according to the model presented in the other chapters of this book. When all of those ingredients are in evidence, it allows an administrator to successfully answer the question the new, larger stage of school leadership poses: "How does an effective administrator ensure the 'whole child' success of all students (including meeting standards) while navigating a world driven by external/outside forces?"

EIGHT
Management

Management: The act or art of managing: control, direction; capacity for managing (*Webster's*).

Effective management is a critical aspect of leadership. The following are examples of effective management.

SAFE AND ORDERLY ENVIRONMENT

At any level, one of the first and most significant responsibilities of a leader is to provide a safe and orderly environment. An orderly environment is one that has clear practices and organized routines (student and teacher schedules, bell schedule, evacuation protocols, etc.) and a clear calendar that communicates events, activities, night meetings, parent involvements, and so forth.

The number one priority in any education organization is that staff and students feel safe and not personally threatened, and that they are able to work, live, and learn in a clean and orderly environment, one that is emotionally, physically, and psychologically risk free. Without those parameters in place, teaching and learning suffer from distraction; they impact the ability of schools to focus on their reason for being. Learning and student success diminish according to the degree of perceived threat or level of an unsafe school.

Leaders at all levels have an obligation to recognize and work to remove anything that endangers the students and employees. The following are three examples of conditions that cannot be tolerated and that the leader must address:

- Bullying: Bullying may be defined as the activity of repeated, aggressive behavior intended to hurt another person, physically or mentally (Besag 1989). Bullying is characterized by an individual behaving in a certain way to gain power over another person. When a person is being bullied, fear and survival take precedence over teaching and learning. Bullying takes place in several interactions: student to student, student to teacher, teacher to student, teacher to teacher, and staff member to staff member.
- Threats to staff (school and association) from anywhere: students, parents, unhappy members, or patrons.
- Disruptive behavior from nonstudents: those people who are not currently enrolled in the school and who come on campus to see friends, intimidate others, carry out illegal activities, or just "hang around."

In addition to safety, there are practical implications for the leader who strives to ensure a safe and orderly day-to-day school operation. Consider these scenarios:

- If the principal is in the building and the fire alarm goes off, if necessary, does he know where the shutoff is and how to shut it off?
- Is there an established, orderly evacuation plan, one that includes a systematic check of the building to determine the level, if any, of a dangerous or threat situation? Is there an orderly plan in place to signal "all clear" and reenter the building?
- If an outside threat is received in a student or nonstudent building, is there a plan to either evacuate or lock down the facility and ensure that all employees are safe?
- Does the architectural footprint and design include *passive supervision*, such as windows and breezeways?
- Does the receptionist feel safe when others enter the facility? Is there a need for some degree of separation from the visitor—a desk, wall with a window, counter with a gate?
- If there is a police action in the neighborhood, does the leader know what to do with students and staff? How to notify parents? Do parents know where to congregate for updated information without unnecessarily crowding or confusing first responders?
- If working in a building that does not house students, are there plans or communication systems to inform and direct employees?

A sense of safety is required so that students can learn, teachers can teach, and certified staff can support and carry out their responsibilities. There are many implications to a safe and orderly environment. An effective leader will recognize these implications and address them.

PROTECT THE INVESTMENT

The leader should have background and knowledge of building safety and maintenance. The community has a significant investment in facilities and equipment. At any level it is the responsibility of the leader to ensure that this investment is protected. The leader must apply an appraising and critical eye when walking the building; taking part in classroom observations or meetings; or conducting regular formal and informal inspections. Consider the following examples, ones that protect the investment:

- Develop the budget with knowledge of the physical needs of the facility. Make sure to monitor the budget and expend the funds within guidelines, goals, and budgeted amounts.
- Work regularly (every other day and at least weekly) with the maintenance personnel and engineer on inspections, getting and giving feedback and alerts to possible issues.
- Conduct regular inspections.
- When walking through the facility for any reason, in addition to recognizing and greeting students and staff, observe the building with a knowing eye for cleaning or maintenance needs.
- Listen to others; take complaints and concerns seriously. Initiate investigation and correct.

THE FACILITY AS A SAFE ENVIRONMENT

Providing leadership and attention to the facility is necessary not only to protect the dollar investment but also to provide a safe and orderly environment. A school or building that is rundown, one where the paint is peeling and the restrooms are flooded, the loose and warped floor tiles are accidents waiting to happen, the heating/ventilation/cooling system is inadequate for the climate of a frigid winter day or stifling heat—these concerns lessen the safety of the building and have a detrimental impact on learning readiness, student success, and employee effectiveness.

When going to class or work, students and teachers should be thinking about their work and the mission, not about the dark rooms, maneuvering through broken halls, or working in a dreary, dangerous facility.

There is also a behavior benefit to maintaining a school facility. Generally, in a well-maintained and clean facility, students and staff will be more likely to take pride in their school—respecting it, keeping it clean—and less likely to vandalize it. When providing a quality environment in which to live, work, and learn, people tend to behave in ways respectful to the facility.

The inverse of both of these is true as well. Students will not fully respect a dirty facility or one in disrepair. They won't think twice about writing on a wall or leaving their trash in inappropriate places if there is already writing on the wall and trash strewn around. A rundown facility communicates a negative message, one that is unhelpful as adults strive to teach appropriate behavior toward the facility, toward each other, and toward authority.

This section is presented with acknowledgment to author Jonathan Kozol, who has written many books cataloging the inability of poorly funded schools and districts to provide facilities equal to better-funded schools and the impact on student learning and morale. Among these books is *Savage Inequities: Children in America's Schools* (Kozol, 1991).

Additional and more recent information on the condition of America's schools can be found in *Condition of America's Public School Facilities*, a 2014 document from the National Center for Education Statistics, U.S. Department of Education. This survey states that more than half of America's schools need repair, renovation, or modernization at a cost of $197 billion.

IMPRESSIONS ARE IMPORTANT

When meeting someone for the first time, the first impression is immediate and lasting. The same can be said about a facility when someone sees it for the first time. The appearance of a facility can communicate a great deal about what goes on inside. Is the facility orderly, thus implying that the programs and people inside are orderly as well? Is the facility organized, easy to navigate, and obstruction free? Is it appealing, cared for, and clean and tidy?

A guest, a student, a parent, a vendor, or any visitor who approaches the facility should see a clean and welcoming facility, a desirable one in which to learn, live, work, and visit. The building should reflect the beliefs and practices that people are cared for and welcomed. The facility many times creates the first impression for the day and for the rest of the time a person is associated with the organization. That impression helps develop a mindset, and it is highly desirable to channel that mindset toward teaching, learning, and respect.

A *safe and orderly environment* and *protecting the investment* include a facility that is clean, appropriately functioning, and risk free. These considerations also contribute to the behavior of the people who spend their time in the facility. A facility that is "kept up" communicates respect to students and others as the appropriate way to behave and treat the building. If students and staff are given a pile of rubble in which to learn and work, the unconscious impression is "this place doesn't care about me." Even if that is not true and in fact the staff does care about the children in its school, an uncared-for facility is just another distraction that must be addressed when attempting to establish positive behavior and attention to teaching and learning.

The exemplary leader is mindful of what the facility represents and acts accordingly.

NINE
Intentional, Analytic Decision Making

Inherent in leadership is decision making; all administrators and school or district leaders must make decisions (although there are some who have trouble with this). It is vital that every administrative leader has a clear concept of how decisions are made. A principal and district leader should develop a structure and process to guide decision making so that decisions are made intentionally and carefully, except in the case of emergencies or the need for an on-the-spot decision where instincts and experience are the guides.

When working with a group, particularly a school staff, the principal should share the model. This is a sample of a decision-making structure and process that includes five options:

1. The staff's decision, no involvement from the principal
2. The staff's decision, input and involvement from the principal
3. A decision to be made equally by the staff and principal, including equal weight votes and input
4. The principal's decision, input and involvement from the staff
5. The principal's decision, no input or involvement from the staff

Decision-making skills and abilities improve and evolve with use; a structure like the one above can become incorporated into a leadership style. After applying over time, it will become mostly unnecessary to think consciously through the five options when faced with a decision. Application of any process will become instinctive, though there will be time to consciously review decision-making options and apply the one that best suits the situation.

While some things are "givens" and do not require a decision (e.g., do not overspend the budget, make sure a teacher is in every classroom), what follows are some of the factors involved when considering which of the five alternative models may be appropriate:

- The ability, confidence, and courage of a leader to analyze a situation or decision and say "This one is mine." Examples:
  - School improvement process
  - Cancellation of an underperforming program
  - Dismissal of a staff member—at any level, including the dismissal of a principal
  - "I am interested in 'this' and I just would like to do it."
  - "I have to take this one. I may not want to, but it is my job."
- Establishing a vision and communicating it
- Trusting that other people are skillful and knowledgeable; knowing their skills and responsibilities and letting them do their work
- Knowing people in the organization; having a knowledge of their strengths, areas for goal setting, and interests
- Knowing and practicing appropriate delegation of tasks to others
- Knowing how to assess progress, effectiveness, comfort level, satisfaction, and morale; intervening when necessary
- Knowing when and how long to be involved and when to begin to disengage
- Having beliefs about the role of the leader and the roles of the others in the organization
- Knowing one's own personal skills and interests and consciously deciding to keep responsibility for some projects based on this personal knowledge
- Knowing what tasks and decisions are appropriate for which members of the organization, including projects or decisions that are more appropriate in the hands of others rather than yourself
- Realizing the leader will be ultimately accountable for the end result
- Knowing how to be involved, monitor progress, and assign final accountability regardless of whether a failure or success
- Knowing to whom everyone is ultimately accountable and maintaining those relationships (superintendent to board, principal to superintendent, teacher and staff to principal, committee to president, association officer and staff to board)

Here are some examples of the five decision-making options, or a combination of more than one, and how administrative leaders might apply them.

As a principal:

- If there is a police action across the street from the facility, there isn't time to call a meeting. Someone has to recognize the issues and take control. The appropriate decision is *option 5*, the principal's decision. There may not be time for input from others. (As an aside, there are situations where the person who takes control isn't necessarily the designated, formal, or structural leader. An example would be when the assigned leader seems undecided or indecisive and a member of the group, one who is not the formal leader, steps up and takes control by organizing and directing.)

- The school receives a bomb threat. It is the principal's decision to evacuate the school. *Option 5*: The principal's decision, no input from others.
- The school will reflect the best middle school practices. *Option 5*: The principal's decision, no input from others. How those practices will be implemented in teams, classrooms, and school is *option 2*: Staff's decision, opinions and involvement from the principal.
- Lesson plans and homework assignments. *Option 1*: Staff's decision, no involvement from the principal.
- Personal and professional goals for the year. *Option 2*: Individual or collective staff's decision, opinions and involvement from the principal.
- Hiring staff. *Option 4*: The principal's decision, input and involvement from the staff, and then *option 5*: The principal's decision, no further input from others.
- Staff evaluation including supervision and discipline. *Option 5*: Principal's decision, no input from others.
- School improvement goals and activities. *Option 3*: All staff's decision, equal votes and input.
- Budgeting. *Option 4*: Principal's decision, input and involvement from others.
- Carrying out agreed-upon programs, approaches, and activities. *Option 2*: Staff's decision, opinions and involvement from principal.

As a central office administrator (superintendent or designee):

- Principal goal setting. *Option 4*: Principal's decision, opinions and involvement from district superintendent or director.
- Safe and orderly school. *Option 5*: Principal's decision, no involvement from district office.
- District goal setting. *Option 4*: Superintendent's or director's decision, opinions and involvement from others.
- Whether to implement a new professional development model. *Option 3*: All district administrators' decision, equal votes and input.
- Hiring of principal and district office staff. *Option 5*: Superintendent's decision, no involvement from others. Perhaps in the case of a principal, it could be *option 4*: Superintendent's decision, search committee input.

As a president in an elected role or a committee chair:

- Determining agendas, assessments. *Option 5*: President's/chair's decision, no involvement from others.
- Scheduling meetings. *Option 4*: President's/chair's decision, opinions and involvement from others.
- Carrying out individual task volunteer work or assignments. *Option 1*: Members' decision, no involvement from president/chair.
- Discussion and determination of committee work and outcomes. *Option 3*: President's/chair's and members' decision, equal votes and input.

As a general rule, when considering the appropriate process to apply to decision making, leaders work with and through others. This is desirable for organizational buy-in, shared investment in outcomes and successes, and utilizing the skills and talents of other people in the organization.

Some decisions in the organization can be delegated and some cannot. Regardless of who is doing the work, the accountability remains with the principal, administrator, or chair. Decisions related to budgeting and school safety are clear examples. These decisions may be made with or without input from others, depending on time. In an emergency situation (e.g., a student altercation, a fire) there may *not* be time and someone has to take charge.

The leader relies on others for successful outcomes, and although the leader remains accountable, some decisions can be delegated. These decisions may be less material or immediate and may be more conceptual:

- Tasks, assignments, responsibilities of staff committees, teams, or departments carried out by the members who will be responsible for completion of the work.
- School improvement processes and changes that must be implemented by staff members who are responsible for not only implementation but also for taking an active role in assessing improvement progress and adjusting when necessary.
- Working to make sure that members of the organization (school, district, committee, association) are successful must be a combined effort and although the responsibility of the leader, others take active roles (department heads, support staff, interested constituencies, and so forth).
- The superintendent has ultimate accountability but delegates much of the responsibility of carrying out the district functions and mission of schooling to other administrators.

Of all the decisions a leader makes, staff hiring and organization may be the most significant, and options 4 and 5 should be seriously considered. If leaders surround themselves with others who possess complementary talents, personalities, skills, and knowledge, and if those others are mission driven and loyal, the organization will stand a much better chance of success.

Accepting that leaders must make decisions and knowing the theories of structures of decision making is the science. Being able to make appropriate decisions, ones that solve problems and forward the mission of the district and schooling (application of decision-making knowledge), is the art.

The science of leadership, in the context of decision making, is:

- Knowing and having a list of alternative ways to decide
- Through observation and other means, being able to obtain the information and implications relating to a situation or problem
- Knowing and understanding the policy and relevant legal codes

Applying all of those appropriately when faced with a decision—knowing how to judge the intensity of a response and understanding the follow-through with constant monitoring and adjusting if necessary—is art.

TEN
Delegating

There are too many people, groups, tasks, issues, and responsibilities in any school or organization for one person to do it all. Successfully working with these multiplicities requires a variety of skills and abilities. In addition to relying on herself, it is through working with other people that the effective leader finds the talents necessary to address the challenges, issues, and work of the organization.

The ultimate responsibility for the school or district rests with the principal or superintendent. Even so, part of working with people is recognizing that others can do things, sometimes better, and letting them do it through delegation and with support. Delegation is not only desirable, it is a significant factor in meeting the demands, responsibilities, and requirements of an organization. Effective delegation draws on and takes advantage of the skills and talents of more than one person.

An example of delegation is the cleaning of the building. Depending on the size of the school and district, the principal or superintendent is responsible for a clean facility but usually is not the person who carries out the work. That work may be delegated to other administrators or the engineering and custodial staff. The principal is usually involved in a supervisory role and becomes directly involved only if additional support, resources, or intervention is required.

The cleaning of a building is an easy-to-understand example, and it results in a benefit to the entire organization. There are many reasons to delegate:

- *Gaining experience and assessing abilities*: A principal may be mentoring a prospective administrator and assign her a specific project. A superintendent may be observing a principal for a possible district position and appoint him to chair a district committee. An execu-

tive director may be considering a staff member for additional responsibility and give that person new and varied tasks.
- *Complementary talents*: An administrative team may have been put together carefully so that the members of the team bring complementary skills to problem solving and operating the school, district, or association. A principal may have good people skills, organizational leadership, and instructional skills, while an assistant is more versed in curriculum design. At the district level, the superintendent has overall responsibility but finds satisfaction in the political elements of the position. Others take responsibility for human resources, special services, maintenance, and so on.
- *Shared responsibility*: The larger the organization, size and logistics require that more than one person be responsible for tasks and outcomes.

There are at least two considerations when delegating. The first is to whom to delegate; the second is to avoid micromanaging.

TO WHOM TO DELEGATE

No one wants to fail; people want to be successful. Most people do not undertake an activity with the idea that they will not be successful. They may have concerns, doubt, or anxiety, but they do want to be successful. In some cases, it is the leader who needs to instill the confidence. When delegating, the leader must believe that the person receiving the assignment will be successful.

How is that determined?

In all cases of working with people, it is paramount to know their strengths, skills, interests, and potential. That certainly is a requirement for teachers (to know their students). Likewise, it is a responsibility that the administrator knows her staff.

An effective classroom instructor demonstrates many characteristics. A few of these are:

- Believing that all children can learn
- Having a solid grasp of subject matter
- Knowing the developmental stages of the age group—the changes and implications for personal growth as well as learning
- Demonstrating empathy and understanding

One of the most important of these is "knowing the students"—their ability levels, interests, current achievement level, readiness potential, and capacity for learning new materials. If the teacher knows these things, that teacher will create progressive, incremental lessons that will lead the student to success through a step-by-step process.

Delegating

The same "need to know" (the staff) is relevant to administrators as they engage in the delegation of responsibility, authority, and tasks.

If a principal or superintendent delegates a responsibility or assigns a project, she should do so with several expectations: that the person will be successful in carrying out that responsibility, exercise the authority appropriately, and successfully complete the project.

Delegation should be exercised with as much knowledge as possible of the person to whom something is delegated. With knowledge of the person and in a mentor relationship, for example, the mentor can gradually assign more responsibility and authority based on the interests, abilities, and past demonstrations of success. For example:

- A conscientious and effective mentor will not assign a curriculum-writing project to a building administrator who excels in student relations and has no interest in curriculum development (unless in a cooperative and agreed on attempt to stretch the administrator or provide a growth experience).
- A counselor who is a prospective administrator volunteers to lead a major school project such as an all-school and community campaign to implement a drug and alcohol program. The principal may first assign the counselor a smaller responsibility, like chairing a faculty study group that is examining the school's homework policy, to determine that counselor's effectiveness and readiness for a broader project.
- A principal has three vice principals, all three inherited from the prior administration. The principal may realize that one of those individuals is a pure curriculum person and does not enjoy nor do well in directive or confrontational situations. That person may not be the vice principal assigned to a teacher requiring intense scrutiny regarding instruction and perhaps dismissal.
- A district office staff administrator, one not in a supervisory role, may be interested in a line position, one with supervisory responsibility. The superintendent should determine whether that person has the ability and capacity to supervise others, make decisions, or sit in review of appeals.

Understanding and knowing the skills, abilities, and potential of those with whom a leader works is key to appropriate delegation and successful outcomes.

Two examples of effective delegation follow.

Example 1: A superintendent knows the board is interested in exploring year-round schooling. At a superintendent's cabinet meeting in August, he shares this information with the cabinet members. A member of the cabinet, a director, has had some experience and interest in year-round schooling and says he's interested and willing to make that research one of his goals for the year. The superintendent agrees and assigns that responsibility.

The director sets his own schedule and plans a report to the board for the following spring, which is timely in the event the board has interest in implementing a pilot project for the coming year. He has a budget and uses part of that budget for attending conferences and bringing in information and resources that provide background and foundation information to other administrators, selected building staff members, and representatives of the board. He updates the superintendent weekly and at the cabinet meetings.

The entire project is his responsibility. He carries it out with no interference; has the support of the superintendent, who is available to him whenever and for whatever reasons; and makes the report to the board in April.

In this example, the superintendent knew his staff. He recognized the director's ability, interest, and capacity for carrying out a major investigative project and allowed him to do it.

Example 2: A middle school principal has several good potential administrators on her teaching staff. She is interested in giving them more responsibility so she can assess their readiness for administration and they can prepare for a prospective administrative position. She is interested in observing how well they accept and handle authority as well as how they perform.

She appoints one of these potential administrators as chair of a parent outreach initiative. Another of these potential leaders is given the task of developing materials for emergency and school evacuation procedures. A third person is given the opportunity to help plan the process, which will result in transitioning the school into a research-based and age-appropriate middle school with knowledge and programs that match the research and age of the students. A fourth teacher is offered the opportunity to sit on a district committee, one focusing on long-range building development. A fifth teacher is given the opportunity to serve as adviser to the student government.

The principal knew her staff—their abilities, interests, and career goals. She generated a list that included several leadership opportunities and then talked with each of her teachers individually. She told them about the five projects and asked whether they were interested in any of them and why. She then made assignments based on the teachers' interests as well her assessment of their abilities and capacity to stretch those abilities to a new level.

In this example, the principal knew that some of her staff members had administrator aspirations. She identified several leadership opportunities and in cooperation with each aspiring administrator she made assignments that matched their interests and abilities. She then monitored, worked with, and supported them as needed, even though it sometimes took more time to teach and support than it would have taken had she done the work herself. By appropriately delegating, important work was accomplished and the principal helped the teachers reach their goals

Some observers of the delegation just illustrated may believe that the principal is simply passing off responsibility and tasks. In some cases of poor administrative judgment, that may be true. However, with appropriate delegation, the administrator is managing to get many things accomplished by trusting her colleagues.

She is giving them an opportunity to learn and grow. She is closely watching and checking in with these budding administrators and at the same time focusing on broader aspects of the educational endeavor by visiting classrooms, working with student groups, and chairing other significant committees at the school and district levels.

Things are getting done, people are growing and learning, and the principal devotes her time to other matters yet continues to monitor the progress and success of the aspiring administrator and the programs with which they are connected.

EFFECTIVE DELEGATION

An administrator is the leader of the organization and must work with people. Those are givens. As an effective administrator leader, an administrator contributes to the success of the organization and of all staff by understanding how to use delegation effectively. The following considerations are important for effective and successful delegation:

- Never forget that the ultimate responsibility remains with the principal or superintendent. That responsibility cannot be delegated; only the processes to carry tasks out can be delegated.
- Work with the person receiving the delegated task to establish timelines. Make sure the timelines are appropriate for the project's deadline and are manageable for the person executing the task.
- Have benchmarks in mind, points at which certain things should be done, ones that match the timeline and reflect progress toward activity completion, and establish those with the person to whom the task is delegated. If something is delegated to a person, particularly if it is the first time or as a growing experience, the principal or superintendent should check in regularly, making sure that things are progressing according to the timeline.
- The administrator should help determine whether there are obstacles and offer advice to overcome them. The supervisor should be continually or at least regularly assessing progress and the way the project is carried out.

- Positive and constructive feedback is important. Reinforce success and good work.
- Be prepared to help, support, and encourage. Provide resources that are needed, or discuss alternative ways to proceed if resources are not available. A person cannot accomplish a task without the needed resources.

MICROMANAGING, OR RATHER, *NOT* MICROMANAGING

Micromanaging can affect a person's effectiveness and morale, impede a person's confidence and ability to perform, and probably will not provide growth and development opportunities for the delegate or contribute to the success of the organization. Micromanaging undermines success. A couple of delegating pitfalls to avoid:

- Do not tell the person how to do the job. Suggestions of alternatives are appropriate, as are ideas for ways to get started. Be available, and encourage updates and the delegate to ask for support if it is needed. However, do not hound the person by checking in every day. Don't insist on written and regular updates unless there is a specific reason to do so.
- Do not intervene if the person is doing something in a way different than you would do it. Let the person do things her way. There may be some small risks and failures. The person will learn from those and hopefully, if the relationship is solid, she will ask for advice or support or ideas.
- The degree of failure and risk to the person, the project, or the organization will clearly dictate the degree of support, intervention, or absence of intervention.

You can sometimes learn lessons by examining processes that went wrong. Here are examples. Can you see where delegation has gone awry?

Example 1: A high school teacher comes to her principal and explains that she is in an administrative preparation program and would like to take advantage of any administrative opportunities and experiences that may be available. The principal offers this teacher a task that has just been assigned from the district. The task is to organize and carry out an evaluation of the need for a summer school program.

The principal monitors her progress on a daily basis, giving advice and ideas that are overly critical and mostly unwelcome and unconstructive. During these daily monitoring meetings she provides unasked for critiques and suggests alternative ways to do things. As the principal observes the progress, she becomes increasingly more interested and involved in it. She takes over a part of the project herself and, to the dismay and disappointment of the teacher, becomes the focal point toward the end of the process and the "face" of the project as it nears completion.

At this point, the teacher, who is looking for administrative experience, becomes more and more disinterested and disengaged in the project. As her ownership wanes and she is gradually replaced by the principal, she spends less energy and time on it. The task was completed, but the delegation to a colleague was handled in a way that did not meet the teacher's goals or the original intent.

Another possible scenario and consequence in this example is that the teacher becomes frustrated by the constant monitoring and unasked for suggestions, ones that are becoming more like meddling than support. She expresses that frustration to the principal, who reacts by shutting down communication. The principal becomes stone faced and walks off in a huff. She makes no further contact with the teacher as the teacher, who is now solely responsible for its success or failure without help or support, carries out the project.

The project is completed, but there are gaps in the study, the conclusions are based on faulty correlations, and the program is not adopted. By completely withdrawing her support and mentoring, the principal contributed to an unsuccessful project and an unsuccessful administrative experience for the teacher.

Example 2: A superintendent was approached by one of his directors with a proposal that he conduct an all-district project. Wanting the director to be successful and believing he could be, the superintendent agreed.

It soon became clear that the director was struggling with the project, both conceptually and operationally. Timelines were not being met, benchmark products were not being produced, staff interest was waning, and feedback was kind but critical.

Still not wanting the director to fail, the superintendent began doing all the planning and idea work, but behind the scenes. He began creating and producing documents and independently altered timelines. He began to give the director very specific and limited directions and activities to carry out as he planned the event and guided it to completion.

The project continued, and at its conclusion the director was given (and he accepted) credit for it. He included it in his resume and a short time later was hired for a position in another district, a position with more responsibility, including the same kinds of tasks the previous superintendent had completed for him. He took the position but was missing valuable experience and was not adequately prepared for it. He had not been successful in similar, prior experiences and may have risked his success in the new position.

Example 3: A principal was known for his narrow range of interests in a school. He attended only to those things that interested him, yet he involved himself in everything by "dabbling." He was not interested in a school improvement project, so he delegated it to an associate principal, a task in which the associate had interest and which he accepted enthusiastically.

The associate carefully and systematically structured study and information meetings, formed a staff leadership committee, and developed other related timelines and tasks. He developed an incremental process. The staff committee was showing interest in and generating excitement for the school improvement process, and progress toward establishing a school improvement plan was moving along nicely.

At a later meeting of the faculty/administrator leadership team, the participants were about to finalize the plan and present it to the staff. It was clear that staff members sincerely appreciated and enjoyed being part of the process. In the meeting, discussion was serious. Academic support and enthusiasm were evident, and there was every reason to hope and expect that the process would result in a school-wide goal, one in which everyone could participate and would support.

Then the principal dropped by in the middle of the meeting. He made a joke about the whole idea of school improvement, laughed at the intensity of the process, and jokingly asked, "Why are you all taking this so seriously?" And, laughing, he left.

All enthusiasm and energy was drained instantly and measurably. The principal's comments were such that they communicated a lack of interest, support, and commitment to the concept of school improvement. The project lost all sense of priority and significance in the eyes of the committee and the faculty. No school improvement initiative was undertaken.

In this example, there was no ongoing micromanaging. However, there was a clear case of undermining and ultimate micromanaging that negatively affected the outcome.

Delegation is important and necessary in any organization. A principal delegates instruction to teachers, and other functions of the school to those with interest and expertise. A superintendent and executive director delegate programs and functions to district and association staff and, in the case of managing and leading schools, to principals.

The science of delegation is knowing that it is desirable and beneficial, both to the organization and in providing opportunities and experiences to potential leaders. A further element of the science is knowing the elements of and considerations related to delegation. To delegate effectively is an art.

Delegation should be based on knowledge of the staff. Although the ultimate responsibility continues to rest with the organization's leader, once someone has been delegated a project or responsibility, she should also be delegated the authority to carry it out with constructive and positive support and mentoring. Responsibility for the project should be with the person assigned to the task. That person has a responsibility to work in collaboration with others, including her supervisor.

ELEVEN
Analysis Prior to Decision Making

Continuum: 1. Something in which a fundamental common character is discernible amid a series of insensible or indefinite variations uniting discrete parts; 2. A continuous series or whole, no part of which is perceptibly different from the adjacent parts (Dictionary.com).

In everyday life, each person faces a variety of decisions. Some are small, require no thought, and may be automatic through repetition (brush your teeth in the morning, drive or take transportation to work, cook dinner). Others may require more consideration, and that consideration requires an examination of consequences and implications (stop after work for shopping but risk being late, apply for a new position but commit to study for the interview and new position if appointed, remodel the house or condo instead of moving but take time to study options, if thinking about a new car talk with automobile dealerships about how that might impact managing the monthly finances).

In an administrative leadership position decisions are daily, and many of them have significant implications and impact—for people and the organization. As an administrative leader is presented numerous and various scenarios, he must first be cognizant that a decision is required. The next step is to decide whether to respond, and if so, what the degree of response should be. For example:

- A principal sees a student start to walk out the door but knows the student should be in class. *Decision*: Intervene. *Action*: Get the student's attention and direct her to class. (Yes, take action. Degree of response is minor.)
- A principal observes part of a lesson during a drop-in visit and sees a way it could be even more effective. *Decision*: Support the teacher by reinforcing what went well and suggesting ways to improve. *Action*: Casually drop by the teacher's room after school, compli-

ment the teacher on a fun and effective lesson, and make a specific suggestion to improve the lesson's effectiveness. (Yes, take action. Degree is minor.)
- A principal sees a teacher in the hall talking adamantly with a student. *Decision*: Don't intervene. *Action*: None, but may be curious.
- A principal receives creditable information from several parents that a teacher is dating one of his students. *Decision*: Intervene. *Action* (a possible but not exhaustive list): Talk with the teacher, report to personnel, talk with the student's parents and the student, report to law enforcement. (Yes, take action. Degree is significant.)
- A superintendent, while in a school, sees a hall sign announcing an upcoming student meeting, but a word is misspelled. *Decision*: Intervene. *Action*: Jot a note to the principal. (Yes, take action. Degree is minor.)
- A superintendent receives a phone call from a board member that a group of parents is organizing to defeat a bond measure. *Decision*: Intervene. *Action* (possibilities): Inform other board members; organize a committee to support the bond; call administrators to determine whether they had the same information; call the leader of the "no" campaign and respond to questions and concerns, ask to speak to "no" supporters. (Yes, take action. Degree is significant.)

Very few decisions are dichotomous; they are not simply yes or no. And very few decisions demand the same level or degree of intense, or minor, response. Analysis first requires awareness of circumstances and settings through observations, then determining a yes/no action in response, and finally determining the degree of significance for that response. Analyzing in the context of degrees (continuum analysis) is a tool that can effectively be used in decision making. A leader can use this process to determine factors influencing a decision, priority, risk, or impact.

The approach to analysis as described here provides a structured process, one that examines the spectrums, degrees, and implications of "maybe" on the yes/no scale of any decision. It provides a method for determining degrees of significance.

While almost all decisions are inherently "maybe," some are not. There is not much "maybe" to consider in embezzling district funds or dismissing a teacher who is selling drugs. In those situations continuum analysis can be applied to the behavior and activities *following* a clear-cut decision, but the initial decision itself is clear.

There are degrees to virtually everything. Laughter. Risk. Danger. Priority. Friendship. Attention. Temperature. Happiness. Conflict. Anxiety. Enthusiasm. Anticipation. Energy. Speed. Virtually everything.

Multiple implications and factors impact every decision. When faced with a decision, thoughtful analysis provides the leader a way to think through the issues affecting it and see how everything affects the final decision or course of action.

The decision maker identifies those issues and assigns a degree of significance to each one. When each individual issue has been analyzed it is then factored into the decision making process, affecting where on the "act or not act," or the "yes or no" continuum the decision rests. It provides information that supports the decision and, once the decision is made, helps formulate the plan to activate it.

Simply put, when a person is faced with a decision, that person asks a series of questions as she analyzes it:

- Here is the situation.
- Is there a need to act? If so, how dramatically?
- What are all the things that affect this decision or will be affected by it?
- How significant (where on its own, individual continuum) is each one of those?
- How does that level of significance impact the decision? Does it bring me closer to a yes or a no or move my thinking one way or the other? Does it guide the degree of how dramatic and substantial the action should be?
- Here is my decision. These are the steps and activities to take in following through with that decision.

The effective administrator will be able to recognize and then analyze a situation, disaggregating it to identify each issue that affects it. Part of that analysis will be to see how every other activity, and its degree along the continuum (people, groups, circumstance), affects that analysis and the ultimate decision and outcome.

The concept of continuum analysis may be employed consciously. A leader may consciously consider implications and the degree to which alternatives impact others and the organization. This conscious deliberation takes many forms. Thinking through the issues may do it. Another way is by constructing a force field analysis and then weighing the significance of each list or items on each list.

In other cases, when analyzing a situation, a leader may trust her instincts as she considers alternatives.

Every situation is different—significantly or slightly—and intentional continuum analysis is appropriate even when two issues appear to be similar. Though appearing to be similar, there will always be major or subtle differences. Examples:

- Two administrators in districts may be addressing the same topic, like deciding how to address a two-person conflict within the faculty. However, in each school, the administrator, the tone of the school, and the people involved in the conflict are different, with

different needs, abilities, backgrounds, and agendas. As such, the analysis will result in different decisions at the two schools, with the approaches and outcomes having varying degrees of impact.
- When discussing a particular child's learning, a principal might talk in one way with the parent and in a different way when consulting with the student's counselor. The issue is the same: the student's success. The audiences are different and require different analysis, considerations, sensitivities, and understanding.
- Gun control in the schools: Discussing this topic with the school board, parent advisory groups, and student government requires different analysis, approaches, and decisions. The same is true when discussing the issue with parents who desire more control in comparison with representatives of the community's National Rifle Association. Again the issues are the same yet require different considerations in the analysis, which results in different approaches.

Continuum analysis—intentional analysis by examining implications, degrees, and impact—is a tool that can be helpful and effective as leaders consider potential courses of action and their outcomes.

DECISIONS—EVERYTHING STILL AFFECTS EVERYTHING

As discussed earlier, the gestalt of leadership is the sum total of many components, ingredients, and elements. The same can be said about decision making. There are hard decisions and easy decisions, but no decision is made in a vacuum. Instead, decisions are made in the context of environment, factors that are in or out of the decision maker's control, and a vast array of influencing patterns and circumstances.

After considering alternatives and the implications of each, ultimately a decision is yes or no and to what degree. On the yes/no continuum there are lots of "maybes." As factors are analyzed, they affect where on the "yes/no/degree of substantial response" continuum the decision rests. These factors also guide the decision maker in determining how significant a response should be.

Here is a simple example of a continuum analysis: Shall I break the law? Yes or no?

On one end of the "Shall I break the law? Yes or no?" continuum is "never." On the other end is "always." Most everyone is somewhere in the middle; very few are at the extreme ends. Most people are not criminals, but rather are law-abiding citizens who value the rule of law. But occasionally something happens, or a decision is made and a law is violated, usually with minor consequence. Who hasn't gone faster than the posted speed limit at some time in their driving career? These sometimes lawbreakers are at the far end of "no" on the "Shall I break the law?" continuum. They are not at the very end, but close.

Though a thought process to break a law may or may not be conscious, there are other factors that may impact a person's decision to break or not break the law. Consider those factors that affect where along the yes/no continuum the decision rests:

- *The driving speed limit*: Is there a medical emergency? How serious is it? Is it a broken arm? Perhaps there is not as great a need for speed. Or is it a heart attack? This would put the answer to "Shall I break the speed limit?" toward the "yes" end.
- *Pilfering a loaf of bread*: What if starvation is close or there is a family that hasn't eaten in two days?
- *Revenge*: Break the law to assert revenge? Maybe, but maybe not. If yes, what might be the severity of the action that would assert that revenge, thus affecting the final decisions of yes or no and how much. He stole my marble, so I'll steal his to get even (exact revenge). That example may result in a yes decision and may be wrong, but it is fairly simple. How about violence with a weapon in return for a violence suffered? Same topic, but the analysis (the risks are too high and the consequences are too severe) probably leads to a different decision and outcome.

The "Shall I break the law?" continuum is a straightforward way to understand continuum analysis—analysis by degree—through a fairly easy question to analyze and answer. When examining the elements surrounding a decision, almost all of them can become complex.

Educators and leaders can use this same analytic approach.

A core educational value, phrased as a question, is "What is best for students?" In education, this core value should be applied to any situation requiring leadership and decision making and be a major, if not *the*, factor in making yes or no decisions. It should be considered in all decisions. In some cases the answer is clear, and in others maybe not so simple. Where on the continuum do the answers fit? What are the elements affecting the situation that help determine where it fits?

Here are a number of examples to illustrate the use of continuum analysis.

Example 1: A principal believes a staff member should be removed. The principal has to decide yes or no to that person's removal. The principal asks, "What is best for students?" In considering the answer, he knows that the teacher is not a good instructor.

In that sense, what is best for the students in the class is removal. That places the decision far toward the "yes" end of the continuum. However, in looking at other factors that make up the gestalt of this leadership activity and decision, other considerations may affect that "yes" placement on the continuum.

Perhaps the school has experienced three critical situations in the past month and is just now recovering from those. Things are settling down a little. One more critical situation (i.e., a teacher's dismissal, with the resulting contract issues, interpersonal conflict, staff members maybe taking sides, union advocacy) might severely disrupt the overall education environment, making it even more difficult for everyone, students and teachers alike, to settle into the business of teaching and learning. Therefore, upon further analysis the principal might ask, "How much damage can this teacher do until a dismissal action can begin at a later time?"

The answer to that question affects where on the yes/no continuum the removal decision lies and what other resources may or should be assigned to support the students. The actual answer may be "no, do not remove the teacher (for now)," but the degree of "no" is more in the middle of the continuum, more toward "yes," when the action to support the decision is to allocate more resources to the class.

A question to ask concerning most decisions is, "How do you assess the overall risk to the organization, and after doing so, how does that impact student well-being and learning? The answers to those questions affect placement on the yes/no continuum. Sometimes the direct answer is clear. It might become less clear when examining the milieu.

Example 2: A staff member has violated both the contract and the district policy. In this case, the yes/no decision for removal is clear, unavoidable, and required. Very little analysis is needed so far. The decision rests at the far end of "yes." But that decision is not made in a vacuum. It is made in a context and has implications. There are decisions that will follow, all of which will need to be analyzed as to degree, appropriateness, risk, and other factors including:

- Investigations
- Suspensions
- Contract and legal compliance
- Communications to supervisor, other administrators, school communities, and parents
- Support for other staff members and students
- Timeline and process for filling the position
- Unknown ramifications of the decision and action

The initial decision is straightforward, but there are follow-up decisions and implications that might not be as clear cut and should be analyzed.

Example 3: A superintendent has initiated several programs, projects, and changes in the district. There is more to do, but how much more can realistically be introduced? Can the principals, board, and community continue to support additional initiatives? The pending question is "Shall we continue to initiate change at this time? Yes or no? How much?"

In making this decision, it is necessary to examine all the issues surrounding the previous changes and the milieu of the district as a whole. Considerations are:

- Is the next scheduled change critical? To whom? (Yes/No/Maybe/Fully or Partially?)
- Has the board added new members? (Yes/No)
- Are there returning or new board members who ran on a platform against more change? (Yes/No/Some)
- Has the community supported or resisted past changes? (Yes/No/Some/What kind?)
- Are the principals effective and loyal leaders who can embrace and implement further change? (Yes/No/Maybe/How much more change?)
- Are the schools effective and stable or are some of them troubled or have wide achievement gaps? Are the principals in conflict with each other or the administration? (Yes/No/Some/Maybe/How much?)

Those considerations would be significant in determining the position on the "Yes or no, Shall we implement the next change and to what degree and how quickly?" continuum, leading to a final decision.

Continuum analysis can be a valuable tool in assessing many aspects of leadership style and processes. Examples of behaviors and approaches that fall somewhere on a continuum include:

- Aggression to subtlety
- Direct/confrontational or rhetorical/subtle persuasion
- Formal presentation to informal table discussion
- Control to delegation
- Immediate action or letting a situation evolve further

Among other examples of spectrums or continuums that examine degrees and would affect yes-or-no decisions, consider:

- Risk to organization (high to low)
- Risk to personal integrity, position, authority (high to low)
- Cause and effect (what other things may happen and to what degree would they affect the outcome or decision)

Continuum analysis is a tool that assesses the degrees of many factors involved in any decision. A thoughtful leader will be aware of the need for analysis and exploring options. She will know that it is important to consider how all the elements in a milieu affect the decision making process. This is the art of decision making, and part of the art of leadership.

AN ERROR OR A MISTAKE?

One last comment on decision making comes from a speech by President John Kennedy, and it may be some of the best advice an administrator receives. An administrator, in his remarks to the faculty at the opening day of school, quoted President Kennedy: "An error doesn't become a mistake until you refuse to correct it." Kennedy realized that as president he may err. However, he also pledged to do everything he could to prevent an error from becoming a mistake. The administrator said that he too may err, but hoped to minimize any mistakes.

Everyone errs. Leaders are in positions where they must make decisions every day. Not all of those decisions will be error free. As a driver recognizes that a wrong turn was taken, he usually makes a correction, backtracking and taking the correct turn or even stopping at a gas station for directions (unless the GPS system makes an auto correct in the routing!). When a leader recognizes that a wrong direction was taken, or that additional evidence indicates a new or different direction is warranted, the leader will admit, at least to himself, that an error was made and take action to avoid a mistake.

An administrator should not be reluctant to realize his own imperfections, and where applicable, correct any errors. This realization is particularly relevant, as there will be times when a leader is faced with decisions that require taking risk.

At times, after all the available information is considered and alternatives and implications factored in, a decision may still not be clear cut. A decision must be made, but each possibility involves taking a risk. By definition, risk contains the possibility of failure or that the decision will not solve or adequately address the problem.

Once a decision is made, especially a potentially risky one, the administrative leader must continually monitor the application and outcomes of that decision. If it begins to appear that the decision will not have the desired outcome, a conscientious and courageous leader will alter, amend, or completely change the decision and direction. An error was made, but by compensating for new information, a mistake was not.

Here are two examples that relate to staffing and leadership.

Example 1: After his first year in the position, a principal was in the process of hiring an assistant, an addition to the administrators' team of the school. The candidates were screened and interviews with finalists conducted. At the end of the interviews, none of the candidates met all the expectations and needs of the position. However, one candidate was on staff and was very popular. He and the staff expected him to have the position. Being one year into the role, the principal, though somewhat reluctantly, named the on-staff applicant to the job.

As he suspected but hoped not, the principal was correct. The new assistant did OK, but he wasn't particularly aggressive or inventive in the position. And most importantly, he wasn't happy. At the end of that year, the principal initiated a conversation with his assistant. He was kind but honest, and pointed out several areas where the assistant needed to improve. He also wondered out loud whether the assistant had the desire or capacity to make the needed improvements. He then offered a specific plan, and as an alternative, a teaching assignment with some leadership components included. The assistant took the instructional position and was happy, and he was an outstanding teacher.

The principal, and the assistant, corrected an error.

Example 2: The superintendent hired a principal without opening the position. He selected from a person in the district thinking, "Who else is out there? No one." The principal had many difficulties with the union, with parents, and with teachers. The principal demonstrated few leadership skills and by most accounts was unsuccessful. Rather than correct the error, the superintendent supported the principal, gave him no feedback, and took no action. The principal eventually was named to a position in another district and left.

By not correcting an error, the superintendent made a mistake, detracted from actualizing the mission of the district and education, and undermined his own leadership.

TWELVE
Elements of Leadership

An important part of the belief system of any potential or existing leader is the knowledge that everyone has strengths and that those strengths are the foundation to success and a person can build on them. As an administrative leader, you must be aware of a person's individual strengths, build and capitalize on them, and address as best you can any areas for increased knowledge, skill, experience, or improvement (see chapter 13, Goals: Planning, Organizational, Individual).

Consider these significant, bold behaviors that exemplary leaders demonstrate and have in common.

GETTING BACK TO PEOPLE

It is impossible to overstate the importance of this simple concept. There is a reason it is listed first.

Imagine the first class in a course titled "Leadership." The teacher or professor begins that course by asking the class participants a series of questions.

First, by a show of hands, "How many of you have ever had an idea or a concern and shared it with a supervisor? Or have you ever asked for a reaction from or forwarded a piece of information to a person in a formal leadership role?" After hands are raised, the professor asks each of those individuals to jot down a couple of words or phrases to remind themselves of their personal experience, the experience of asking something of their supervisor, and tells them that the class will come back to this in a few minutes.

Second, again by a show of hands, "How many of you have ever had *someone else* come to *you* with an idea or a piece of information? A concern? Asked for reactions?" Again, after the hands are up, they are asked to jot down a little reminder.

Third, the professor takes them back to their examples and asks them to write down what happened during the following twenty-four hours in regard to the communication, both when they approached someone and when someone approached them: "What follow-up took place? How did you feel about the follow-up? What were your impressions about the follow-up you received or the person you talked with?"

Following those three questions, the professor asks a few volunteers to read their responses. During the discussion that follows, it will undoubtedly be revealed that, in regard to the first question (when the students shared something with a supervisor), there likely would not have been any follow-up in the first twenty-four hours following their request.

In discussion about the second question, the professor asks how many of the class participants themselves followed up within twenty-four hours. Did they take the other person's feelings into consideration? Were they concerned about making sure the other person was recognized, heard, or validated? Did they respond within twenty-four hours, and if so was it for shallow reasons like "get it off my to-do list?" Or was it for more affirming reasons like "I have a personal policy to not let things go too long," or, "The person expected and needed a reaction and I wanted to make sure he received one?"

After discussion, the professor writes four little words on the board, ones to live by: *Get back to people.*

It is a constant source of frustration and disbelief, and it is confounding that, in all aspects of life, more people do not see the value and power in the application of those four words.

Getting back to people is a vital behavior, one to which every leader should religiously adhere and conscientiously and consistently employ. Immediate confirmation, with either an answer or a comment like "I need additional information," or "I'll be back to you on this tomorrow," or "I can't get to this right now, but I won't forget and I'll be back to it as soon as I can, no later than Monday," will communicate so much more than just the content related to the issue.

Getting back to people removes ambiguity from their lives and allows them to focus on their primary responsibilities and objectives. Plus, it validates them. Their idea or question will be deemed significant and they, in turn, will be deemed important. When a leader *gets back to people,* these people do not have to ask themselves or wonder:

- "I wonder if by asking that question, I look dumb."
- "The leader *never* gets back to people or follows up. Why should we bother to report that a student or teacher is at risk."

- "I wonder how I am being viewed or discussed since I asked that question. What is she telling others about me?"
- "I sent that student to the office last week. I wonder what happened; should I ever do it again? Under what circumstances?"
- "Was my question not important enough, or am I not important enough to warrant a response?"
- "I'm the principal and I have a situation. I informed the superintendent two days ago and have not received feedback, a policy explanation, a yea or nay . . . nothing."
- "As a board member, I sent the executive director an agenda item and a concern. I guess it wasn't worth considering because I haven't heard back. But it is important, at least to me and my constituents."

Among the threads that connect leadership in all dimensions and categories, this is a central one. Getting back to people is critical for many reasons and a value and practice that an effective leader must know, apply, and believe in. Knowing it is important may be part of the science and knowledge base of leadership. Doing it in a timely and effective way is part of the art of leadership.

VALUING INSTINCTS

Instincts:
A natural or innate impulse, inclination, or tendency (*Webster's*).
A natural aptitude or gift (Dictionary.com).
A natural aptitude, impulse, or capacity. A complex and specific response by an organism to environmental stimuli that is largely hereditary and unalterable, does not involve reason. (*Webster's*)

Valuing instincts is one of the more clear examples of art in leadership. Everyone has instincts, and they are a part of everyday life. They play a constant role in leadership behavior. For example:

- In a meeting, it may be a feeling a person gets, one that influences and guides a reaction to a statement or behavior. A person who is new to the group and is usually quiet offers an idea. The leader instinctively responds in a supportive and gentle way, one that may be different from the way she responds to a regular and long-time member of the group (one the leader knows is a frequent contributor), and as a friend.
- In planning a long-range project, the leader senses that the project could go in several different directions depending on circumstances. That leader works, following his instincts, to ensure the project progresses in a way that best meets the goals.

- When faced with a decision, it may be that one course of action "feels" better than another, even perhaps when information or logic dictates otherwise.

Events and issues have different degrees of importance and likewise, some decisions will have varying degrees of impact and importance. Additionally, leaders take varying degrees of risk when acting on instincts. For exemplary leaders, good instincts are part of the art of leading—an innate, natural ability that sets them apart from scientific leaders, ones who were trained or taught to be leaders. An exemplary leader:

- Knows her instincts and when to listen to them
- Is in tune with his instincts
- Has a record and high degree of success when trusting them
- Continues to trust them
- Acts on them when she instinctively knows it is the best or the right course of action

What are good instincts? The criteria are most likely found in past effectiveness—a track record. Has past instinctive behavior resulted in successful outcomes? Or has it resulted in disruptive, unsuccessful outcomes? The following examples illustrate instincts:

- A teacher in a classroom may respond instinctively to student behavior in a variety of ways: ignore it, use it as a teaching moment, or administer some degree of verbal correction. Some teachers instinctively know whether student behavior is disruptive, a sincere inquiry, indicative of loss of interest, or some other manifestation of student attitude or thought. Instinctive teachers know, without thinking, how to respond. A good instinct may simply be to smile and move on. Another teacher may be less secure or not really know the student and ask the student to leave the class. In this case, knowing which instinctive response is the correct one will be determined by both the future relationship with the student and the student's success in the class.
- A team member is attending a team meeting. The conversation is moving smoothly and toward the desired outcome of most members. During this discussion, one of the team members makes a comment completely off the subject. When it is pointed out that the comment is off topic, the team member instinctively stands and leaves the room or blurts out an angry response. This disruptive, unproductive behavior is also the result of instinctive behavior, but does little to contribute to the success of the team, the topic, or the meeting. It is the team member's instinctive behavior, all right, but the instincts are unproductive, especially if it is a pattern—those instincts are not good.

- A project director knows that the project has reached an important point, a point at which a decision must be made determining its future direction or whether it has a future at all. With all the information and evidence at hand, and with several groups advocating and supporting different alternatives for the project, the leader must decide on one. In many ways, all choices have equal support and value. The project could go in one of several directions or be brought to an end. One of the alternatives just feels better, and the leader guides the project in that direction. She trusted her instincts.

These three examples demonstrate how instinctive behavior can support or inhibit success. Exemplary leaders have a diverse set of experiences and a positive record of instinctive behavior that is helpful and contributes to successful outcomes. Colleagues who know and have worked with the person will share that judgment and trust future decisions. By trusting instincts, and with a track record of success, instincts help set an exemplary leader apart from other leaders.

As it is phrased in the vernacular, though somewhat roughly, "trust your gut." To that it is appropriate to add, "That's good if you have trusted it before and things turned out OK."

COMMUNICATION IS CRITICAL: WRITTEN, SPOKEN, INTERPERSONAL

All leaders must be effective communicators. Through communication, leaders:

- Impart ideas and other information clearly
- Motivate
- Demonstrate expertise to obtain credibility
- Understand people
- Move groups and people toward desired goals

An effective leader must know how to clearly express ideas both orally and in writing. When addressing an individual or any size group, a speaker must know how to gain and maintain attention, relate the material to the audience, and develop a structured and easy-to-follow presentation.

There is an artistic element in working with individuals and groups. An effective leader must be able to observe and interpret verbal and nonverbal behavior and determine appropriate responses such as changing course, reward, acknowledgment, sanction, and feedback. A leader may also need to ignore these behaviors depending on other elements in the milieu, the people involved, and the purpose and goals of the meeting.

KNOWING WHEN TO ACT ... AND WHEN TO WAIT

Anticipation and fear of the unknown create varying degrees of anxiety. Often, particularly as a leader, it would be easier to "get it over with," or move quickly and get it done—avoid the uncertainty. As desirable as that might be, sometimes there is just not enough information, and taking action would be premature. *A leader has to know when to act and when to wait.* Gallup's SRI Administrator Perceiver calls this *ambiguity tolerance* (Gallup, 1979). A leader has to be able to live with a situation until there is enough information to make the best decision. Although there is no room for hesitation in an emergency, most situations are dynamic and fluid, and by waiting, additional information will surface and the decision can become more clear. In other words, "Sometimes you just have to let it play out a little longer."

The anxiety resulting from not knowing sometimes influences when action is taken. The decision made today might be different from the decision made tomorrow or next week after the leader had waited until knowing more. Everyone has some degree of ambiguity tolerance, a lot or none, and everyone lies somewhere on the "ambiguity tolerance" continuum. Many times, it is beneficial to have more tolerance—and to wait.

This is not to suggest that waiting is always best or to ignore the fact that waiting too long can turn into paralysis and indecision. Sometimes that may be a symptom of ineffective leadership. Making a hasty decision can be detrimental, but so too can it be detrimental when the leader *can't* make a decision, when no action is taken, and the organization becomes staid. That is not ambiguity tolerance. That is ineffectual leadership. The exemplary leader will know about and consciously be aware of ambiguity tolerance, apply it appropriately, and instinctively know when and for how long.

BEING OBJECTIVE

Everyone brings bias, relationships, and history into every situation. To be fair and to analyze effectively, a leader will view situations and make decisions with some degree of objectivity. Objective analysis is critical during decision making. It is important to put aside negative feelings, feelings about other people, past unpleasant experiences, self-enhancement, and other factors that may influence judgment. By viewing things objectively, it is easier to make the most appropriate decision. Of course, the degree of objectivity that is desirable depends on the issue, the situation, and the milieu.

For example, knowing the research and benefits of middle school programs will appropriately bias the leader toward implementation. However, to enhance the success of the implementation objective, a conscious approach is required. Decisions should be made regarding when, how, and whom to involve in the implementation, and those decisions should be made objectively. The leader may want to begin immediately, but an objective view of the staff and school may slow things down to prepare everyone and gain their commitment to the work. One of the best staff members needed to begin the work may be overcommitted. An objective view may realize this and a second, less committed person may be selected. Understanding the theory and elements of objective analysis is scientific. Applying them is artistic.

THE COURAGE TO DO WHAT'S RIGHT

Decisions are made in response to issues and events. For each decision, some degree of courage is required. Some decisions are easy, routine ones that require little thought or analysis. However some decisions will demand a great deal of thought, consideration, planning, and introspection. The actions and possible outcomes may be highly stressful, demanding, and risky. When faced with those kinds of decisions, a leader will not necessarily or consciously consider how much courage may be required or needed, but some courage will always be needed.

Thinking in terms of cause and effect and answering these questions will help determine degrees of courage:

- What are the implications of this decision? Who and what is affected?
- What are the risks? Personally? Professionally? To the organization?
- Does the decision I'm going to make sufficiently overcome the consequences of the risks and other implications? Is this the right thing to do in spite of everything else? Where is the balance?
- Does this decision require any courageous stands or risks? Now or after it is announced or implemented?

After considering all the implications of a decision, judging it by many other factors, and moving the answer one way then the other on the continuum, a final decision must be made. Then a final question: "Do I have the courage to make this decision and live with it *and* the outcomes and implications?"

ORGANIZATION TO GET THINGS DONE

All leaders work with myriads of issues, tasks, responsibilities, and people, all at the same time. Organization is an important skill that contributes to establishing priorities, both immediate and long range. Organization also contributes to making sure things get done and people are responded to in a timely way. Motivated leaders can learn the science—the techniques—to facilitate organization. Some examples of strategies that contribute to effective and organized leadership are:

- Prioritizing tasks
- Keeping lists
- Taking time to think through a meeting agenda—possible directions the discussion may take, dynamics of the participants, potential outcomes
- Keeping a calendar
- Generating timelines
- Disaggregating large tasks into smaller, interdependent ones
- Assigning tasks
- Listing tasks for follow-up

The following is an example of an organized approach to one element of instructional leadership—teacher supervision. This structured approach makes sure that tasks are accomplished within expectations and timelines and that each staff member is valued.

At the beginning of every year, a principal created a supervision spreadsheet. On the left-hand side of the spreadsheet he listed all the staff members for whom he had responsibility. Across the top of the spreadsheet he listed all the events that he wanted to accomplish with each person. For example:

- Goal-setting meeting
- Formal observation including follow-up conferences
- Informal observations including feedback
- End-of-year evaluation conference

There may be other items to include, but this is a start.

At the beginning of each week during the year, the principal took out his spreadsheet and identified what he wanted to accomplish in the coming week and with whom. For example, at the beginning of the year the week's goal could be "conduct six goal-setting conferences." After the goal-setting conferences were completed, the next week's goal might be "conduct formal evaluations, two staff members each week."

He would place in the selected staff member's mailbox a notice of the scheduled observation and conference date and time, a request for lesson plans, a request for anything special that the teacher would like to be observed or noted, and the time and place of the postconference. He scheduled them and added them to his calendar and weekly goals. And he made them a priority.

He sent out the appropriate notes, memos, and notifications. Then he conducted the observation and held the meetings as scheduled. For an upcoming observation or meeting, many teachers will be somewhat nervous and will take extra time preparing their lesson. The teacher may also be anxious about the follow-up conference, both looking forward to it and relieved when it is over. This principal never disappointed them by canceling or postponing the observation or follow-up conference. That is significant, as canceling or postponing not only results in a letdown and disappointment, but it also communicates a lack of priority and importance.

This kind of forethought can be applied to any position of leadership and to almost any task or responsibility.

This approach to organization is concrete and sequential. Regardless of the processing style, organization is a key factor in successful leadership. It is a tool and attribute that makes sure things get done. People process and organize in different ways. Exemplary leaders work to discover and identify what organization techniques and styles suit them best; then they strengthen them and capitalize on them.

THIRTEEN

Goals

Planning, Organizational, Individual

When responsible for any organization, an administrative leader must know that circumstances and environments are constantly changing. People and institutions must change with them to continue moving forward, not backward. The principal or superintendent is responsible for making sure that adapting to change is part of the fabric of the organization. This begins with a vision and is actualized by a strategic plan.

STRATEGIC PLANNING

On a Monday, a couple invites two other couples for dinner, arriving at 5:00 p.m., on the following Saturday. The vision is to have a nice evening with friends. The goal is to have a welcoming home with a flavorful and impressive dinner. Depending on the organizational ability of the host couple (Courtney and Brett) and the degree of formality desired, they will conceive and implement a strategic plan. For example:

- *Wednesday*: (Courtney and Brett) Talk and decide on the menu. Determine the cleaning that needs to be done to ready the house.
- *Thursday*: (Brett, who is the cook) Have the shopping list completed: crackers and cheese or hot snacks and dip, drinks, salad, main course, dessert. Do preliminary food prep with the veggies.
- *Friday*: (Courtney) Pick up accessories after work. Candles, napkins, table and living room decorations.
- *Saturday*: (Courtney and Brett) Clean the house and address any needed issues. (Courtney) Set the table. (Brett) Set out cookware.

Do preliminary food preparation with vegetables. Chill the wine, soda, beer.
- *Saturday afternoon, 4:30 p.m.*: (Courtney) Have preliminary snacks ready to serve. (Brett) Begin prepping the prime rib for roasting, set the oven to preheat.

The above steps are an example of a strategic plan familiar to most people. Though simple, it contains all the elements of strategic planning. Other typical, frequent examples might be planning a multiyear program for a graduate degree; planning a graduation celebration, a wedding, or anniversary event; completing holiday shopping; organizing children's school events; or executing weekend chores, job catch-ups, or home remodeling projects.

Side note: A reader familiar with either strategic planning or an event similar to the one outlined above will immediately notice the missing step. Even a strategic plan may not be complete, and when a step is missed, this error may significantly impact the event. (Hint: When was the grocery shopping to be done?)

A strategic plan is more than a set of ideas and goals. A strategic plan has specific tasks that are broken down into actions, responsibilities, timelines, evaluation, and redesign. A strategic plan must be specific, measurable, and fluid without losing its mission foundation.

A strategic plan includes vision, goals, and specificity. These are three separate entities.

- The vision is created and established by the principal, superintendent, or executive director. A vision, or part of a vision, may also originate from another source such as the school board or other individual with standing within the system. Eventually, however, to be realized, any vision must be embraced by the leader of the organization. The vision is shared with other stakeholders and work begins.
- The next step is that goals and ideas are generated. These goals and ideas are ways to realize the vision. (This step is as far as some organizations get. They never go to the next step or in adequate detail.)
- Developing specific plans is the final step. These plans are the ways that goals are realized and implemented. Each goal should have its own plan, one that includes detailed activities, timelines, and the person responsible for making sure each activity is completed. These plans *cannot* be too specific.

A more complex sample strategic plan, one containing vision, goals, and specificity, can be found in appendix 1.

ORGANIZATIONAL GOALS

The smooth day-to-day operation of any institution strengthens the organization. Teamwork improves, and people become more predictable in the way they respond to each other; routines can be established, put into operation, and not have to be reinvented; and interactions with students, staff, and other personnel can enhance relationships. However, institutions mustn't become stagnant or stand still. Actually, there is no way they can stand still, for if they don't improve they will decline. Change is inevitable. Organizations and institutions must have focused, intentional plans to adapt to the changes around them. Simply stated, the institution must have goals that align it to a dynamic environment.

The following information illustrates each step of the three-phase strategic planning model.

Vision

Every leader should have in her mind a picture five years into the future. The leader should picture how the organization should function, what it should be doing, how it is responding to the mission. This vision is general and largely unchanged. It undergoes monitoring, assessment, and modification (by the leader and key advisers and participants) as needed. Examples:

- Our middle school climate and programs should reflect attention to the developmental needs of the age group. The programs should be selected and implemented based on student development stages and middle school research.
- Our district should have in place an effective school improvement process in each school. Each school should have a principal who exhibits all the qualities of an exemplary leader.
- The district will have in place the beginnings of the basic elements of the Common Core Curriculum.

Ideas and Goals

To realize these visions, steps should be taken to identify obstacles. Ideas and goals should then be generated, ones that address those obstacles. Here are obstacles, ideas, and goals that would address the visions as used in the examples above:

Middle School

- The curriculum is not sufficiently aligned and integrated to provide subject matter connectedness and relevance to the students. *Goals*: Provide the staff with resources that support integration; provide

the staff with information and training that helps them develop curriculum integration; provide the staff with time to plan and introduce their approaches to integration in their classrooms; provide time for reporting, feedback, and adjustment.
- After conducting a student survey it was discovered that students don't feel involved in developing their own educational goals. Student participation in and ownership of their learning are important factors in middle school education. *Goals*: Conduct research to find schools and programs that involve students in planning their learning goals and objectives. One possibility might be student-led goal setting and conferencing. Introduce the idea to key teacher leaders and then to the entire faculty. Establish it as a school goal and provide training and time for implementation.

School

- Some principals have no training or background in school improvement practices. *Goal*: Provide principals with school improvement models and background through readings, resources, and discussions with other principals engaged in school improvement; provide for observations of other schools' leadership team meetings; provide any other materials and resources they identify and request. Establish the expectation that each school will engage in a school improvement process; monitor the implementation.

District

- Some principals are unfamiliar with the Common Core Curriculum as are some teachers. There is confusion and outright negativity regarding the Common Core Curriculum in some of the parent communities. *Goal*: Provide training and professional development for administrators. Create a district Common Core Curriculum Committee for intense professional development and training to help them teach and support others. Administrators will provide training for their teachers. The district and each school will organize and conduct community information and feedback meetings.

Action Plans with a High Degree of Specificity

The final step is developing specific plans, and it is through implementing these plans that anything gets done, in a systematic, progressive, and effective way. These plans include specific activities, specific timelines, and accountability—the individuals responsible for each activity. The following is an abbreviated list of specific activities for a few of the visions and goals just listed. This list is not comprehensive or complete.

Additionally, there is a partial strategic plan, including specific activities, included in appendix 1.

Middle School

- The principal will form an in-school committee to coordinate the curriculum activities. It will have met once in December (completed by winter break). Prior to that, she will discuss the goals with the leadership council and ask for their suggestions as to who should serve on the committee (October 1). An announcement will be made to the staff regarding the committee and its goals. The announcement will ask for anyone interested to see the principal (October 15). All names will be listed and the leadership team will discuss who should be appointed (October 25).
- The coordinating committee will be provided with a list of conferences and resources and a budget (December 15).
- The committee will discuss the resources and make recommendations to the principal (January 20).

District

- The superintendent will ensure his own knowledge of Common Core (July 31). He will include an administrator assessment of Common Core understanding at the administrator in-service (assessment tool finalized, August 15; administrative in-service, August 20).
- After analyzing the results (September 1), the superintendent will present them to the administrative team (September 15) and ask for their input and ideas for providing more information about Common Core and how to provide in-service for faculty.
- Ideas are finalized and first administrative in-service is held (October 15). Principals will prepare an in-service schedule (including the action plan and specific activities) and review them at principals' meetings and with their supervisor (November 5). The plan must include ways to present information to faculty in small groups and parent information meetings.
- After discussions (November 5) and following the completion of the first of the administrative in-service meetings on Common Core (November 30), all plans are finalized (January 5).

These are just a small sample of the specific activities that any action plan must contain. The list will go on and be more expansive, and each building principal will have her own list, one that relates to the individual school and meets the district goals that would realize the vision.

A consultant was conducting a two-day workshop on strategic planning for a state-wide association. There were thirty people from across the entire state. After introductions and reviewing the agenda, the consultant stated, "Thirty hours from now you are going to hate the phrases 'be more specific' and 'more detail.'" It took thirty-four hours, but toward the end of two days, with focus on discussion, development, and reporting of action plans, the participants did finally become a little irritated and impatient.

That doesn't matter. If a goal is going to be realized, it can be realized only through a specific set of activities, timelines, and designated responsibility.

SOURCES OF INSTITUTIONAL GOALS

Institutional (and individual) goals usually originate in three ways:

1. The principal, superintendent, or executive director has a vision for the organization and sets into place goals and ideas to realize that vision.
2. Data that demonstrate areas for needed improvement. For example, a school improvement data analysis may reveal the need for emphasis on an across-the-curriculum reading program or a spring/fall transition program for incoming students.
3. Those that are imposed on the institution by legislative or policy makers. A district or school board may impose an expectation to improve student success as reflected through test scores. Legislative mandates or judicial decisions may impose goals related to student discipline that will have implications for replacing past practices or adopting new policies and procedures.

Regardless of the origins of the goals, it is the process in reaching those goals that is important:

- Create a vision
- Identify the obstacles or problems
- Generate plans to remove those obstacles to realize the vision

Just as having institutional goals is vital for school improvement, so too are personal goals an important element of self-improvement. Both are evident in the exemplary school and the exemplary leader.

INDIVIDUAL GOAL SETTING

No one is perfect. Everyone has strengths and areas that could be strengthened. An exemplary leader will recognize this in himself and others and conduct goal setting accordingly.

An individual's daily activities comprise one form of improvement. It is progressive, but often passive. Experiences will be banked and can be called on and applied to future situations. In addition to experiential growth, it is important to have focused, conscious, considered, and targeted goals.

Things change. Each year presents a new set of circumstances, new information, changing conditions. This requires an ongoing process of and adjustment in individual goal setting. Last year's goals may have been met, may no longer be relevant, or, after evaluation and adjustment, may continue into the coming year.

Considering a hypothetical need for changing attendance boundaries, the following may be appropriate individual goals:

- *Superintendent's goal:* At the beginning of the year, the goal is to manage the process leading to recommendation for boundary changes, involving all the constituencies. At the end of the year, the boundary change recommendations are made, adopted, and completed. Plans will need to be developed for transportation, staffing, and distributing information to the constituents. However, for now, at the end of the year, the superintendent's goal is no longer relevant for the next year. A refinement of the goal might be to monitor how students and parents are adapting.
- *Principal's goal:* Determine the demographics of the new incoming students and provide the staff with in-service activities that will help them serve and support those students in their adjustment to their new school.

Other examples of individual goals might be something in which the administrator is interested, like exploring student learning styles and using that information for staff in-service presentations or activities, or exploring a grant opportunity and attempting to generate resources that would fund a technology program.

Another consideration of individual goal setting is self-improvement. Though some would have you believe they are, no one is an expert on everything. As circumstances and considerations change and new and updated information is constantly generated, every administrative leader should be continually thinking about what would make her more effective:

- Read more information on instructional leadership. Keep updated in technology.
- Explore how other schools work with students in the age of technological devices and social media.
- Research the latest and most effective observation tools.
- Initiate a "Future Leaders" program for both students and teachers.
- Become updated in school reform, year-round schooling, or an innovative community connection program.

- Return to school for a doctorate, an additional license, or to pursue a topic of interest.
- Explore other roles in education—university teaching or charter schools.

As with organization goals, each individual goal will require a plan with specific activities and timelines, including benchmarks. This plan cannot be too detailed. To have a goal with a general idea for how to achieve it is not enough. Realization of a goal happens through specific activities.

Different conditions in different schools, districts, and individual situations may result in very different kinds of specific goals for different administrative leaders.

During a summer at a social gathering of friends, all of whom were administrators, the conversation found its way to the topic of goals for the coming year. Many of the administrators had lofty and important ones, personal and professional and institutional goals. One of the friends, a vice principal who had just experienced a tumultuous year with a highly ineffective principal, had goals too: "stay out of trouble and learn to make soup," although school and education goals should probably be somewhat less humorous and more directed to improvement. This vice principal was attempting to navigate troubled waters in his school and with several other colleagues. (As a follow-up, that administrator did learn a lot about himself and accomplished a considerable amount during the subsequent year. The following year he was appointed as principal.)

HELPING OTHERS

There is one other dimension of goal setting, a responsibility of leadership, and one that can be both science and art. It is helping others set goals so that people may be continually updated and successful and realize their career ambitions. In most cases, goal setting with others is a cooperative and supportive activity. Here are some examples of helping others set their goals:

- A supervisor uses the end-of-the-year conference to set the groundwork for the coming year. This can be with each teacher, administrator, or staff member, depending on the supervisor's role. This conference should include time on the agenda for discussing the coming year. The supervisor takes notes, summarizes the notes, and provides copies for the person and the file. Asking questions like the following will prompt responses and information that can be included in conference notes and can be referenced in the goal-setting conference the following year.

- Are you thinking about things you would like to change or improve?
  - Are you planning to work on an advanced degree or license?
  - Where do you see yourself in five years? Let's look at some things that might help you get there.
  - Here are some things we talked about over the year. Think about these, and perhaps we'll incorporate some kind of goal in the fall.
- If there are district goals or school improvement goals, add those to the discussion. Every person in the organization is responsible for working to realize overall goals established by the school leadership team, the school board, or the association board.
- One principal suggested that each staff member come to the goal-setting conference with goals in two categories: (1) a professional one, such as increasing the use of multiple groups for learning or a process that would further the school goals for the year, and (2) a personal, professional one, such as completing the requirements for a master's degree. This took an interesting turn because some came to the conference with *highly* personal goals. Those goals were helpful because the principal was able to understand, support, and counsel those staff members, but they did not necessarily lend themselves to formal goals in a professional sense.

Every supervisor and exemplary leader should know the staff well enough to be able to identify strengths and areas to be strengthened. Everyone wants to be successful, and if the supervisor can see a way to help a person to do that, it is important to discuss those ways. The discussions may or may not result in establishment of a goal, either this year or in a coming year, but the discussion can be supportive and helpful. That discussion would be different (subtle, directive, or collaborative) depending on the staff member and his overall effectiveness.

In some cases, a goal may be imposed on an underperforming teacher, administrator, or staff member. Those goal-setting activities are for one of two purposes: (1) to motivate and direct for the benefit of the organization and thus the students, and (2) to direct improvement, which, if not met, may lead to dismissal if a person is not responding to needed improvement or if it doesn't appear that the person is willing or able to accomplish needed improvement.

Goal setting has many facets, each having implications for the organization and the individual as well as for supervision. Goal setting is an important and significant element in the gestalt of leadership. Knowing this and the theory and elements of goal setting is science. Applying those theories and that knowledge effectively to improve the organization, others, and self is the art.

FOURTEEN
Power

An earlier quotation from Dansby Swanson is worth a reminder: "I found that the best leaders are the ones who are servant-based first. There is a difference between leadership and authority. Authority is more of a title, whereas a leader is the one who is always helping someone first. I think that gets lost in translation these days. Just because you have power doesn't make you a leader" (Quick 2015).

Any formal or informal leader possesses some degree of power:

- An influence over others through personality
- An influence on agendas and programs
- An influence over other people's work, goals, dreams, and ambitions

An administrator acting as a mentor once said, "Keep the title plate 'Principal' in your bottom desk drawer. Take it out only when you have to address an issue for which you have responsibility, such as putting an end to insubordination, stopping an ongoing argument, or tempering reactions over a decision that has already been made. Once or twice a year, you may have to pull out your title. However, the more you pull it out, the less effective it will become."

For the designated leader, the power that comes with the position is authoritative. The formal, authoritative leader with the power to make final decisions, determine direction, and evaluate staff should use that power sparingly. She will be much more effective if she applies influential leadership skills and works with people as opposed to ordering them about or issuing directives.

Administrators who use the power of their office frequently do not enjoy the same degree of support and respect of those with whom they work as someone who uses that power less often. Their power is taken seriously, but as respected leaders they are taken less seriously.

All members of the organization know that the power rests with the designated leader. Exemplary leaders use the power of their office infrequently. They don't need to. They rely on other leadership attributes, skills, and abilities. As a result, when they do exercise the formal power of their office it makes much more of an impact; the action is received with more attention and viewed as a significant message rather than "just another edict." How the leader uses power will determine whether he is liked, respected, seen as a leader, or willingly followed.

Power can be used directly or subtly. For example, *where* and *how* the leader interacts with others is a subtle form of applying power. If a leader requests or directs a one-on-one meeting, how and where it is communicated reflects subtle or direct use of power:

- A casual comment in passing asking to "drop by when you have a minute" suggests something less formal than a note in a mailbox that says "Please meet with me on _____."
- Meeting in a classroom, office, or work space communicates a different message than meeting in the principal's or superintendent's office.
- If a meeting is in the leader's office, the seating arrangement communicates different messages. If the principal is sitting at his desk and invites the other person to sit across or next to the desk it communicates something different than if the principal sits at a round table and invites the other person to join him.

A principal or superintendent can also apply power simply and subtly by her presence. Knowing that a discussion is taking place, informal or formal, and then arriving and observing the discussion shows interest and subtly applies the power of leadership. Attendance lends the discussion an element of importance because the principal or superintendent would not spend time on an unimportant meeting or discussion. Her presence may impact the content, process, and tone of the discussion.

If a leader organizes a group and then agrees to also be a participant, this communicates a degree of importance just by being involved. On the other hand, if the leader does not participate, her lack of concern may minimize the importance of the group's work.

By attending events and activities and being involved in the processes of the organization, the designated leader lends the authority and power of the position to those activities, communicating importance and validity.

Another example of the subtle use of power comes from participating in a study group, committee, or discussion as an *equal member* of the group. If the principal or superintendent is respected others will listen and consider his comments. A part of that respect will come from past experience with him, experience that tells the group members that there will be no arbitrary decisions made nor will there be overrides of their decisions unless for political, legal, or other valid reasons.

As an equal member, the leader contributes ideas and suggestions and helps move the group forward. Unless it is a part of the understanding and need, the leader does not assume a dominant role or make the final decisions. The committee chair or study group leader fills that role.

Recognizing that power exists in the designated leader's hands, there are very appropriate ways to apply power to make the organization productive:

- Approving ideas and requests, and allocating or finding the needed resources by using the power of the office
- Affirming others as they compete and do good work
- Basing yes or no responses (the exercise of power) on knowledge, experience, and priorities; working to make sure others understand the reasoning as well as the decision
- Taking sides on an issue, a dispute, or a conflict and making the decision based on facts and past successful experience
- Intervening in a situation that is destructive or out of control, like a classroom disruption, a physical altercation, or other chaotic or dangerous condition

Though an exemplary leader will be more trusted and the school and staff and relationships will be more collegial if the assigned authoritative power of the position is used infrequently, certainly there are times when it is necessary to invoke the authority that comes with the designated position of leadership. Sometimes it is necessary to overtly assert the power of the position. Some obvious examples are:

- Making a decision about hiring and dismissal and having the authority to do so
- Enforcing policy and law in the face of someone who may resist
- Stopping ongoing questioning and debate on a decision that has been made and is final
- Directing resources in emergency situations

Through personality, past experience, relationships, and implied power an effective leader will be able to work with others collegially and toward realizing the vision without having to state the obvious: "I have the power." However, some leaders know they have the power, do not know how to activate people or planning without it, and use it more often than they should, decreasing its effectiveness. And theirs.

A few examples of the poor use of power by using it too frequently are:

- Saying "because I said so" every time someone disagrees

- Issuing edicts and directives through daily or weekly memos
- Having no variety of strategies or ways to interact with others—using only "the desk between us" approach or the arrogance of attitude and talking down when in discussions or private conferences
- Spending most of the time in the office and not interacting with others in their work spaces
- Providing continued "no" responses to requests, ideas, and suggestions for improvement—of anything, without reason or rationale

Lastly, there is the unethical application of implied or overt power. A well-known and all too frequent example of this is sexual or workplace harassment, situations where the authority figure uses implied or overt power for sexual favors or to address a personal slight or dislike. A few other examples are:

- Misuse of facility and other organization resources either for personal gain or preferential treatment of others
- Misuse of resources due to not being aware of their appropriate use or because of not paying attention or ignorance
- Use of funds for personal use
- Promotions or demotions based on interpersonal relations
- Continued withholding of pertinent information needed by others to complete their work
- Ignoring policy or law either through neglect or ignorance
- Consciously ignoring or refusing to get involved in legal, legitimate organization activities and goals

Power has direct and implied strength, and although not necessarily a science, it comes with leadership and is part of *that* science. How it is used to move the organization toward realizing the mission will determine its effectiveness and the effectiveness of its user—the artist.

FIFTEEN
Meetings and Agendas

Ninety-nine percent of all administrators begin their careers as teachers. Though their direct contact with students is significantly reduced, they continue to remain teachers. Their impact on students and contributions to the mission of education continue in a more general, broad role.

As teachers become administrators, their world moves from the classroom into settings where meetings are conducted:

- Principals meet with teachers, parents, and other administrators.
- Superintendents meet with principals, the board of directors, parents, and community groups.

An effective administrator or institutional leader must accept a world of meetings, know how to plan for them, be able to distinguish one meeting's purpose from another, and effectively conduct, lead, and facilitate them. This involves working with others, and the success of any leader is realized by her ability to do so.

Meetings have different purposes. An effective leader will know the purpose of a meeting, which may be to solve a problem, develop or finalize a project or plan, explore ideas or exchange thoughts, brainstorm, listen, plan for a decision or course of action, or only to decide on a future meeting.

KINDS OF MEETINGS

The number and kinds of meetings for administrative leaders are extensive. Here are a few examples.

For principals:

- A one-on-one meeting with a teacher may be for the purpose of mentoring, or as a follow-up to a teaching observation, or to discuss a student. The meeting may be informal and for the purpose of relationship building and getting to know more about the teacher; it could be more formal as with meeting for a disciplinary reason.
- Faculty meetings have different purposes. They may be social; they may be called to relate information or to listen to feedback. They may be for professional development or problem solving. As a general rule, the larger the faculty, the less effective meeting for problem solving will be.
- Parent meetings have a variety of purposes. Purposes may be to involve the community in the school or to air a grievance or a concern that the parents or community perceives. Another may be for planning and developing ways for the school and community to work together. A parent or community member may drop by unannounced, requesting an appointment or an immediate meeting, one with an undisclosed topic or agenda.

For superintendents:

- Meetings with building administrators or district office administrators may be to discuss programs for which others have responsibility: principals' councils, special services, or guidance and counseling. Many of these meetings will be for the purposes of information sharing or problem solving. However, some of them may be more individual or directive such as principal or other administrator evaluation. Other examples are to discuss options for addressing a student, school, or parent issue or to discuss a parent complaint involving a staff member.
- Board meetings exist to discuss a variety of community, educational, or policy issues: to provide updates such as contact negotiation status, discuss budget or staffing concerns, discuss issues in the community, or review policy background and recommendations.
- Community group meetings may address specific issues such as long-range building plans, a controversial reading requirement, or or curriculum content.

REASONS FOR MEETINGS

In addition to the many kinds of meetings, meetings are scheduled for a variety of reasons.

- *Delivery of information.* Faculty meetings are usually used for the delivery of information. Many times, this information can be written and given to the staff so as to not take up time; then the meeting could simply provide highlights or headings, which are included on a written agenda. Important items, ones that require emphasis, can be covered in more detail during the meeting. For example, in one faculty meeting prior to the opening of school, the faculty was anxious to start work in the classrooms. When it came time to review the newly revised student handbook, the principal simply highlighted a few key changes and asked everyone to read it on their own time (this was greeted with applause). The principal then moved the meeting on to the topics of a pending district grade-level configuration change, school goals for the year as determined by the school improvement leadership team, and related staff issues that were to be addressed in the coming year.

- *Problem solving.* Depending on the size of the faculty, problem solving in a faculty meeting may or may not be appropriate or effective. Large groups can provide feedback, but to facilitate effective problem-solving, smaller groups could be established. Each group would meet within a week and generate ideas and comments, and all groups would share the outcomes of their discussions with the entire faculty at the next meeting.
- *Leadership.* A principal or superintendent usually meets with his assistants and others in the leadership team. These are individuals who have a broader view of the school or district, ones that a classroom teacher or other staff member might not have. These meetings have multiple purposes: discussing upcoming events and issues; checking and monitoring progress in long-range, ongoing projects; assessing student learning, the morale of the staff, or the tone of the school or district; or planning for future in-service activities, school improvement, or other upcoming or ongoing projects.
- *Involvement.* Regular meetings such as these are important so that the combined thinking of the administrative team contributes to decisions and direction. It also keeps the team members involved and invested in the work of the school or district.
- *Disciplinary.* A principal or superintendent may need to meet with staff members to discuss circumstances in relation to reports or events. These may be for updates or to explore possible responses and actions. Or they may be for disciplinary reasons. Meetings like this are person to person, as are meetings for goal setting and evaluation. If the meeting is for a disciplinary purpose (for the purpose of verbal or written reprimands, which may be placed in the staff member's file) they are often attended by an objective observer and an advocate or representative for the staff member. Policies, laws, and handbooks must be followed in these meetings.

Those are only a few of the kinds of meetings and their reasons. The principal, superintendent, or executive director is usually the person responsible for planning and conducting them, and all meetings should begin with a plan in mind.

LEADERSHIP ROLES

Knowing the purpose of the meeting and having in mind the roles and responsibilities of the participants, including knowing who will make the final decision, allows the leader to determine her role in the meeting:

- If it is an information-gathering meeting with a decision to come later from the group or the administrator, the principal or superintendent may assume a listening and facilitation role, not necessarily a role that leads the group to a decision.
- An input meeting with a decision needed immediately will call for a directed and condensed approach. The administrator may assume a more focused and directive role.
- In a meeting for the purpose of discussing curriculum content with the staff members, ones who are the content, subject matter, or integrated team experts and will ultimately decide the content within state and district standards, the administrator may assume a role of participant and helpful contributor.

WHO CONDUCTS MEETINGS

An administrator may or may not conduct all meetings that he attends. A principal may be a part of a faculty discussion group led by a teacher team leader. Principals may attend meetings that are conducted by a director or the superintendent. Any administrator may be a participant in meetings made up of state and national colleagues and are conducted by someone else. Here are a few options regarding who conducts meetings:

- Assign someone else to conduct the meeting, such as a staff member or other administrator. This allows the leader to listen and consider. Some principals assign vice principals to conduct faculty meetings so they, the principal, can be active listeners and participants in significant discussions on major issues.
- The principal will conduct some meetings. When the principal conducts a meeting, it may communicate a higher degree of importance to the topic or group, lending the influence of the office to the topic.
- A principal or a superintendent meets with a staff member, one he supervises such as a teacher or principal. In these meetings, there may be many subjects to cover. The supervisor will conduct the

Meetings and Agendas 105

meeting in a supportive and helpful way or, if the meeting is for the purpose of correcting behavior, be more directive.
- A staff member may be asked or assigned to chair a study group, a school project, or an initiative.
- At school board meetings or association board meetings, the board chair conducts the meeting. The superintendent or executive director and her staff provide resources and can offer guidance. Their influence has been applied prior to the meeting. Decisions and directions are now up to the board.
- An administrator may conduct a meeting and provide direction but leave the decision to the committee members. An example here might be a school improvement leadership group that will be analyzing school data and determining values and priorities. The principal will support the work and decisions, but the collective group will establish school goals.

It is important for the person who is planning and conducting a meeting to know the purpose of the meeting, who will be involved, and where the decision will be made. Knowing these things in advance will be helpful in determining her individual role, could be critical to setting tone and structure, and helps her decide how and whether to conduct the meeting.

FUNDAMENTAL SKILLS

Style, personality, and artistic ability affect the leader's ability to effectively conduct meetings. Regardless of differences in style, there are some common, fundamental skills of which to be mindful:

- The leader must ensure that interpersonal communications are valued and used:
  - Listening to and respecting each other's comments
  - Disallowing participants to interrupt one another: "Excuse me, but I don't think Ron had quite finished his thought."
- The leader should listen carefully to every contribution and keep the discussion on topic. He should not allow himself to be distracted or to engage in private sidebar conversations when a meeting participant is speaking. He shows respect for each speaker through active and attentive listening.
- The leader should be able to appropriately determine when it is time to move the discussion on: "I think I just heard two comments that repeated earlier contributions. Are there any new ideas or thoughts? If not, let's move on," or, "Let's have two more responses and then move on."

- The leader should take notes that include the meeting, agenda topics, discussion summary, highlights, suggestions, and decisions:
  - This allows her to verify or correct any other accounts that may surface later.
  - It provides information for correcting the minutes or writing a draft document summarizing the meeting.
  - It answers questions for others who may not have taken notes.
  - The leader who takes notes and provides the summary influences the subsequent discussions and decisions. This influence is by providing tone in the written account.

AN ART

Art: The exercise of human skill; method, facility or knack (*World Dictionary*).

There are several scientific elements to meetings. The prior pages describe some of those: *Roberts' Rules of Order*, note-taking skills, and techniques for creating agendas and feedback. But no matter who leads it, there is also an art to effectively conducting a meeting. The style and approach will change depending on the person or the need, but regardless of style and approach it is necessary to know when to apply the science and when to:

- Let the discussion unfold. At the initial stages of problem solving, for example, it may be best to just let the meeting participants brainstorm or share their own thinking and ideas.
- Redirect to the main topic if someone has a contribution that is leading the discussion in a very different direction. A way to refocus the discussion is to say, "I'm not sure how that relates. Could you explain?" or, "Good point, and I'd like you to remember that and bring it up in a minute. For right now, let's stay with the main issue, which is _____."
- Take control or refocus. A meeting may digress into two or more people talking at once, become emotional or confrontational, or recycle the same points. Stopping discussion and gaining control of the meeting will allow the leader to refocus the group and discussion, summarize, and move on.
- Soften the mood, tone, or intensity and when to raise it.
- Instinctively know when to end discussion and move to decision making by assessing the discussion and declaring or suggesting a consensus; by taking a vote; or by using other forms of decision making such as going around the room and asking each person for thoughts and her or his vote or using the "Fist of Five" process.

Note: The Fist of Five is a process used to reach consensus or agreement. A decision is almost made and a direction is proposed. The leader asks everyone in the group to hold up a hand with one to five fingers showing:

- Five fingers indicate complete and enthusiastic agreement. The person will work hard to implement the decision and convince others of its validity.
- Four fingers indicate agreement, but with some minor questions. The person will certainly not attempt to obstruct the decision or its implementation if the group decides without addressing those minor questions. The person will be supportive of it.
- Three fingers indicate that the person is almost in agreement, but has a few questions or concerns to address before going to four or five fingers. The person will not disagree if the group makes the decision this way.
- Two fingers indicate serious concerns; the person cannot support the decision, but will not impede implementation if the decision is made this way.
- One finger indicates strong disagreement; the person will not take part in any implementation, and will attempt to dissuade others if the decision is made this way.

An effective leader continuously observes the members of the group, determining their levels of comfort or understanding and reactions to comments and direction, and absorbs and processes the information he observes, information that comes from the reactions of the group members. Instincts and meeting goals direct the leader's responses.

The effective leader has a variety of roles available to her and knows which ones more appropriately apply to the meeting and the conditions:

- The meeting may need firm and structured guidance so that it moves along expeditiously and with progress or doesn't spin out of control. Examples that may require a more firm moderator role include a contentious board meeting, an irritated parent group, or a massive agenda that needs to be covered.
- The meeting may be for information gathering or problem solving, and the leader listens to discussion, letting it go where it will but keeping comments on topic and asking clarifying questions when necessary.
- If the meeting is personal and one on one, unless it is for disciplinary purposes, the administrator can be less directive and authoritative and engage in interpersonal exchanges, being supportive and helpful, more as a colleague.

Some projects require multiple meetings. These projects appear as agenda items in a variety of meetings and over an extended period of time.

The projects and the agenda items are ongoing, such as progress on a budget issue or a request of information on a project as that project evolves. In the case of multiple meetings, the person leading the project, and the person who is usually conducting the meetings, must know where the project is in terms of its progress. The leader must also know what he wants to accomplish by bringing up the project during the meeting. The leader must be able to play whatever role is appropriate to accomplish what is needed for each agenda item.

For example, the first meeting of a long-range project may be free flowing as ideas are generated, problems are identified, and alternatives and directions are explored. The person leading the meeting facilitates brainstorming, idea exploration, discussion, priorities, and analysis. Subsequent meetings may be more focused, calling for a more directed or structured leadership and facilitation as conclusions begin to surface and are leading toward finalization.

REACTING TO DOCUMENTS

At times, it will be more efficient if the meeting participants can react to a draft or a prepared document from the meeting chair or principal rather than having to create it during the meeting. It may be more helpful and effective if a draft, position paper, summary of a past discussion, or some other written document is presented by the chair or principal; then the group may provide feedback, final editing, and agreement. An effective leader will know which is more appropriate. Examples include:

- A principal was presenting a new idea to his leadership team. In a written document, as a way to get discussion started, he presented a need/solution position paper.
- A principal met with her building advisory team members as they prepared to develop a response to the district budget reduction directive. Each team member came prepared with suggestions and the discussion covered them all. The principal took notes, generated a complete list of all the suggestions and their cost factors, and presented it at the next meeting for reaction and finalization.
- Knowing that the board was interested in taking a position on a community issue, the superintendent prepared a draft document for the board members to read, amend, and either adopt, reject, or send back for a rewrite.
- A superintendent asked the district administrators for their thoughts as she considered a directive from the board, one to increase the use of technology in the classroom. After listening to everyone's ideas and asking them to write a brief summary, she combined the summaries into a single document for the administrator group to discuss, review, and finalize.

- An executive director listened as the association board discussed the need for long-range, strategic, ongoing planning. After the board members exhausted their ideas, the director said she would have a document for the board's review at the next meeting. That document was presented, explained, and amended, and the board adopted the amended version.

AGENDAS

Agendas are helpful because they provide an outline and preview of the meeting content. They provide structure for the leader and participants, a structure that contributes to assessing timing and progress toward ending the meeting.

Preparing an agenda depends largely on the kind of meeting and the goals of the meeting, and it can appear in many forms—separate and individual sheets, viewed on a large whiteboard for all to see, or distributed electronically with each person bringing his or her own copy. In the case of a small group, an agenda can be communicated verbally at the beginning of the meeting: "Today I hope to discuss and cover _____."

The *first consideration* in preparing an agenda is the purpose of the meeting. For example, a one-purpose meeting might be to discuss the coming year's school goals. Though the purpose of the meeting is single fold, the agenda might include multiple items such as progress data from the prior year's goals, background on prior goals, reports of progress from individuals or groups, a review of the goal statements, discussion of upcoming programs to meet the goals, and questions.

If the meeting is multipurpose, each purpose should be an agenda item and listed separately. There may be subtopics to support each of those separate agenda items.

A *second consideration* in generating an agenda is soliciting agenda topics from the meeting participants. Sometimes it is appropriate to ask those attending the meeting whether they have anything to add to the agenda. The principal or superintendent may ask each of his leadership team or cabinet members whether they have items for the group. A board president or chair may ask the board members whether they have items for the meeting. An executive director will ask the staff whether there are issues to discuss at a director-level or all-staff meeting. In an association, the executive director will work with the president to generate the board agenda and may ask the association directors whether they have anything they think should be included.

An organized administrator will keep an ongoing list handy on a computer or desk notepad, or use some other form of daily reminder. Another source of agenda items is from the administrator's personal list, one that he revises daily. The list will include projects, subpoints or topics related to them, issues, to-do's, and reminders. As each meeting approaches and the administrator prepares the agenda, he should check the list and include on the agenda anything that is relevant to the group.

A *third consideration* is the meeting time frame, the amount of time allocated for the meeting. An effective administrator prioritizes the agenda; allocates an estimated amount of time for each item; and monitors the discussion and time, bringing discussion to a close, summarizing and calling for a decision, or deferring a decision with placement on future agendas for further discussion and moving on to the other agenda items as needed and as time demands.

Some agenda items are ongoing. For those items that are carried over, and as new ones surface, the following is an organizational technique. This is an excellent way for an administrator to keep track of agenda items in upcoming meetings:

- Keep a file folder for every upcoming meeting either electronically or in hardcopy.
- At the end of each meeting, review notes, minutes, and recollections.
- For an item that should be included in the next or some future meeting, make an entry in that future meeting's folder, adding anything that needs to be included when the agenda is finalized.
- When it comes time to prepare the agenda for an upcoming meeting, review the notes and reminders in that meeting's file folder.

Agenda items come from a variety of sources, and the administrator and leader of the organization will take responsibility for knowing how to form an agenda, whom to include, and how to make the agenda work for the success of the people involved and the project.

HOW ARE THESE ABILITIES ACQUIRED?

A legitimate question is "How does an aspiring administrator learn these things? How does one develop the skills for conducting meetings effectively?" After training and study, there are at least three other factors: The first is experience. The second is instinct. The third is that just as some people can paint a masterpiece, write an inspiring novel, play a musical instrument, or think sequentially or randomly, so too can some people naturally possess the artistic ability to conduct, lead, and guide a meeting.

There are many meetings in the life of an administrator, and they all come with the expectation and desire to further the mission of education. Meetings encompass a multitude of groups and individuals and a range of purposes. The effective administrator will accept meetings, use them to advance the mission, and work with the people who attend them to be productive and effective. Administrators should know the purpose of each meeting they conduct and have a repertoire of personal leadership behaviors available in conducting them.

It is critical for the person conducting the meeting to know the art of meeting leadership: when and how to apply preparation, influence, direction, and intervention.

The tone, interest, involvement, and participation levels of a meeting are dynamic, always changing. The individual conducting the meeting must be able to adapt to the changes, moving with, adjusting to, and guiding the meeting as it ebbs and flows. The ability to do that is an art. Without it, too many meetings become unproductive, and in some cases, boring, unnecessary, and counterproductive.

SIXTEEN

Future Leaders

A Program to Identify, Recruit, and Prepare Prospective Administrative Leaders

Mike Scott

It is imperative that educational leaders work to identify and mentor those individuals who have demonstrated a desire and ability to lead. Failure to develop succession plans leaves to chance the highly important job of leading schools and positively impacting future generations of students. While the importance of developing future leaders is widely recognized as a best practice, the existence of formalized programs within school districts to do this is fairly uncommon. Deliberate and specific efforts to identify, encourage, and develop leaders are essential for staffing our schools with bright, prepared, and natural leaders, ones who will greatly contribute to the success of children and education.

The Hillsboro School District is a district of nearly 21,000 students near Portland, Oregon. In Hillsboro there is a deliberate effort to continually identify and develop those people with the potential to lead. Open to in-district licensed staff who have demonstrated leadership potential, this yearlong program provides participants with a combination of release time and volunteered time dedicated to taking the future leader through a series of experiential and substantive activities.

FUTURE LEADERS

The Future Leaders program has a long history in the district and is led by the superintendent and members of the executive leadership team.

The Future Leaders program exists because the district believes that it is responsible for developing the next generation of administrators who will lead in Hillsboro and beyond.

This program recognizes talent, provides renewal and affirmation and career opportunities, while providing continuity and effective leadership to schools with leaders who meet the goals, expectations, and standards of the district.

IDENTIFYING POTENTIAL PARTICIPANTS

In Hillsboro, it is the expectation of the superintendent that the administrative team continually be working to identify those with the potential to lead others. This stems from the belief that the current leadership team is oftentimes in the best position to identify and encourage future leaders. Annually, all administrators in the district are invited to nominate individuals who they believe possess the necessary leadership attributes and might be potential, effective administrators. When identifying participants, the administrative team is asked to nominate individuals who have demonstrated skills in the following areas:

- Desire to lead and provide service to others
- Culturally competent and committed to equitable outcomes for all students
- Problem solving
- Coachable
- Possess high integrity
- Ability to serve as a change agent
- Strategic decision maker
- Ability to read others—high emotional intelligence
- Effective communicator

While it is true that the Future Leaders program works to develop these skills, the preexistence and recognition of these skills by others is crucial as a starting point for success.

Throughout the fifteen years of the existence of this program, participants have shared that the nomination they received for the program was a pivotal moment for them—a moment that communicated to them that their principal believed in their skill set and potential. Many future leaders share that they had not ever viewed themselves as leaders or future administrators until they began to receive encouragement and recognition for the leadership contributions that they were making at their individual schools.

The leadership team in Hillsboro believes that it is the responsibility of leaders to assist others in recognizing the leadership potential that may possess. While this sounds like a simple and obvious concept, leadership skills may go unrecognized or untapped if it weren't for a deliberate attempt to harness this potential.

When nominating participants for the Future Leaders program, it is not necessary for the individual to possess all of the attributes previously listed. In fact, it is highly unlikely that this will be the case. The goal is to recognize those people with some demonstrated potential in these areas. While it is not necessary to possess all of the skills initially, it is imperative that they have, at some point and to some degree, exhibited a natural instinct for leadership. Further, either consciously or naturally, without a desire to make a greater difference as well as to lead and influence others, the development of a broader administrative skill set will not by itself be adequate in developing a potential administrator candidate.

If nominees do in fact possess these core attributes, further conversations and participation in the program will assist in developing the skills or determining that they do not possess the requisite proficiencies to move into a district administrative position at that time. Regardless of the outcome of the process, it is commonly agreed that participation in the program assists in a greater understanding of their own individual abilities as well as a deeper understanding of the district culture and the administrative skills necessary to be successful within that culture.

Following the nomination of the individual to the Future Leaders program, the executive team reviews the submissions, gathers additional information, and narrows the list to twenty-five to thirty participants. Once the participant list has been determined, the nominees receive invitations to participate in the program directly from the superintendent. The invitation shares the purpose of the program: "a voluntary program designed to help prepare selected teachers who have an interest in administration for future administrative positions."

Additionally, the invitation lists the benefits of participation including that of increased visibility, leadership training, interaction with current administrators, and the gaining of experience. It is important that the initial communication with nominees does not "oversell" participation in the program or guarantee a future administrative position. The goal of this communication is to manage expectations while simultaneously affirming effective previous work and building enthusiasm for participating. With this as the goal, early communication with participants clarifies what the program is and isn't.

WHAT IT IS

The Future Leaders program is:
- A voluntary program
- For those interested in a leadership position
- For those who have the support of a current administrator

- Increased visibility
- Expanded opportunities
- Leadership training
- An opportunity for interaction with current administrators
- A discussion around relevant leadership topics

WHAT IT ISN'T

Equally as important in the communication is what the program isn't. Future Leaders is not:

- A guarantee of an administrative position
- A "sit-and-get" environment (active participation is expected and required)

It is important to communicate this early in the process. Nearly 60 percent of the administrators in the Hillsboro School District were former participants in the Future Leaders program, so it may appear as if this is a virtual gateway to an administrative job. Yet while participation exposes hiring decision makers to candidates' strengths, it also highlights potential limitations and shortcomings.

ELEMENTS AND CONTENT OF THE PROGRAM

Once the Future Leaders candidates have accepted the invitation, they are exposed to and involved in three elements of the program:

1. *Seminars:* This component provides the participant with an understanding of district culture, leadership skill development, and practical skills. Additionally, items such as budgeting, communication, human resources, navigating conflict, and understanding politics will be covered to provide insight into the skills necessary to be a successful administrator in the Hillsboro School District.
2. *Administrative experience:* This component allows for current Future Leaders participants to gain administrative experience by providing opportunities to engage in administrative activities including substituting for current administrators and exposure to experiences/scenario activities that will expand their current skill set.
3. *Oregon Leadership Network (OLN) participation:* The OLN works to build leadership around educational equity issues. Future Leaders are invited to attend two workshops during the year focused on increasing equitable outcomes for students. While considerable attention is focused on this throughout the program, participation in OLN connects Future Leaders to a wider state network of individuals working to improve instructional experiences for students.

Content for the Future Leaders program has evolved over the years. What has remained a constant are timely and relevant topics that are currently impacting the Hillsboro School District. Topics typically discussed include the following:

- Decision-making parameters—constructing criteria and processes for decisions that need to be made as administrators
- Year one—what to expect as a new administrator
- Navigating politics within the school, district, and community
- The change process—managing effective change
- The staffing process—hiring, scheduling, and personnel assignments
- Crisis management
- Communication skills and processes
- Student management
- Staff evaluations
- Staff discipline
- Difficult conversations
- Changing demographics
- Leadership and ethics
- School improvement and change
- School finance/budget development
- Instructional leadership
- Staff development and supervision
- Legal and policy issues

Additionally, it is important that participants be exposed to a variety of practical scenarios that allow them to project themselves into the position they are striving for. These scenarios build confidence and inspire conversation that hone decision-making skills and critical thinking. Examples of scenarios that participants are exposed to include:

- Dealing with an employee who has been inconsiderate and hostile during a staff meeting
- Responding to an upset parent who believes that his or her child is being discriminated against by a teacher because of her race
- Responding to a directive from the district office to increase the engagement of minority parents
- Investigating and suspending a high-profile student
- Instituting a controversial curriculum change

A final goal of the Future Leaders program is to prepare participants with the personal insight and reflective skills necessary to assume a leadership position. This is accomplished through assisting Future Leaders with the construction of their educational vision and the backward-mapping skills necessary to reach that vision. To this end, time is allocated to discussing the steps necessary to create momentum through a greater understanding of how to build a collaborative culture and by understanding how to effectively utilize the formal and informal leaders in the school.

The Hillsboro School District has developed its Future Leaders program over several years. Initially intended to address and satisfy staff members who were curious about or interested in exploring administration, it has also been pivotal in providing leadership to the district—leadership that supports and provides continuity to the visions and philosophy of the district and community. The program has been instrumental in exposing administrative candidates to the values of the district. Additionally, those charged with hiring administrators have gained greater insight to candidates due to their involvement in the program. The program has been deemed successful in all manner of written and verbal evaluation—participant feedback, the number of participants promoted to administrative leader positions, student and staff feedback and success, and parent satisfaction with their schools and administrators.

It is incumbent on those who currently possess administrative roles to make certain that they are developing the next generation of educational leaders. This is accomplished through carrying out our duties in an exemplary manner and mentoring others in a deliberate manner. If we, the current leaders in education, are interested in and committed to providing continued leadership to education, it is an obligation to not only serve in the present but to do whatever is necessary to provide for the future. The Future Leaders program is one way to contribute to that.

SEVENTEEN
The Administrative Interview

While leaders can be effective in any educational role, to be the *most* effective, a person usually attains an administrative position. This can be quasi-administrative (teacher on special assignment, learning coach, attendance supervisor, etc.) or as a member of the administrative team in a school or district (vice principal, administrative assistant, principal, staff or line administrator at the district level, superintendent). While the quasi-administrative position may be attained by appointment or filled without opening the position to multiple candidates, most formal administrative positions will involve an interview.

Interviewing for a position within the district where a candidate is currently working means the candidate is probably known and the interview is a formal step in the process of filling the position. However, many interviews take place with a person or committee *outside* the current employment district, and the interview and the paperwork and references are the main and significant factors that determine who is hired for the position. Knowing that, it would seem that any aspiring administrator would want to prepare for and have a successful interview. There are ways to help ensure that the interview is enjoyable and successful, but that preparation involves several elements.

Before discussing the preparation steps, it is important to note that a successful interview does not necessarily ensure selection to a position. In the overall application process, if a candidate clears the paper screening, is advanced to the final three or four candidates to be interviewed, is confident that she did her very best in the final interview, and presented herself as knowledgeable, poised, and articulate, then the candidate has done all that she could. The final selection becomes a matter of the interviewing team determining the appropriate match for the district, the position, and the needs of the school and district from among the finalists.

There is no way to predict or prepare for the appropriate "match." Match depends on many things, some of them unimaginable and within the milieu of the employing district. These things include:

- A member of the interviewing committee may have had a conflict with someone in the district or on the committee, and that *other person* may be supporting you.
- The interview committee is made up of representatives from every aspect of the school and district: licensed staff, administrators, teachers, classified staff, union representatives, parents, and others. Each person is looking at each answer hoping to hear a particular response, and some of those may be in conflict.
- One of the members of the committee may have had an unpleasant phone call or experience just before joining *your* interview, an experience that did not take place prior to other interviews. That may cloud his attention or receptiveness or filter the responses. There is just no way to know.

The following is an example of something unimaginable and within the milieu of the employing district.

A longtime and successful administrator was sharing interview experiences when he was first applying for principal positions. He was employed as a vice principal and enjoying a successful administrative career, and his current district was in a suburban setting. He applied to a nearby but much more rural district, and was selected for an interview. The interview went well. He thought he connected with all members of the interview committee, and his responses demonstrated knowledge and ability, vision, and leadership. When the call came from the superintendent, he was surprised to hear that he had not been chosen for the position.

To adjust for further interviews, he said, "I felt good about the interview and thought it went well. Can you give me some feedback?" The superintendent was helpful and willing to respond. In essence he said, "Your interview was great. All of the interview committee members were impressed and knew you'd do a good job. They know that someday you will be a successful principal. We wanted to hire you, but one thing was of concern. When you asked about the district and what the district was looking for at this time in a principal, one of the board members, a local strawberry farmer, was talking about the community and funding. He mentioned that there was a drought and as a result not one berry had been picked so far this year, and it was June. When he said that, you smiled. In discussion afterward he said that because you were coming from a nonrural setting, he was concerned that you'd laugh at the farmers and community members."

And that was the deciding factor for filling the position. Match. And who could have predicted that?

This chapter will discuss intellectual and speaking preparation for an interview. It will not discuss interviewing tips. There are many articles and Internet links that address things such as dress, arriving early, a trial run to the interview site a day prior to the interview, or turning off all devices (not just silence, as a vibrating device can be heard in a quiet room).

The following process is related to a person seeking a principal position. By easily adapting it, it could also be applied to a vice principal position and any district office position, including a superintendent. In the case of a superintendent, there are additional factors to consider such as the demographics of the community and board members, the history of the district, and bond and budget issues and needs.

THE THREE STEPS OF PREPARATION

Anyone who has been successful with presentations or taken a speech class in high school knows that making a presentation in front of an audience, either small or large, can be a challenging, rewarding, enjoyable, and sometimes anxiety-producing experience. So can interviewing for an administrative position. As with a speech, there is no substitute for knowing what you believe, preparing in advance, and practicing whether it is the first interview by a teacher for an administrative position or an incumbent administrator interviewing for a promotion or other administrative position. The interview is crucial in the application process and often is the single most influencing factor in selection for a position. The interview should be approached with confidence and a command of the topics to be covered.

The following model is thorough and has proven successful for several administrative candidates. This model was developed to ensure that an applicant could converse knowledgeably and confidently on a variety of topics. When followed, it will work to reduce the tension and nervousness that inevitably result from anticipating an interview. The process does this by instilling confidence, which comes from preparation. Following this process will result in a comprehensive awareness of administrative issues and questions and instill a sense of security that the applicant can respond effectively to any question by connecting personal knowledge and beliefs to that question in an interview setting.

Philosophy

"To thine own self be true," advises Polonius to his son, Laertes, in Shakespeare's *Hamlet*. While this is good advice in all situations, it is particularly applicable to preparing for an interview. The implication here is that one *does* know oneself and is aware of her individual philosophy in regard to children, education, teachers, teaching, and learning.

The first step in preparing for an interview is to know and be able to articulate and communicate what you believe. To do this an applicant should write out (yes, *write out*) her statements of beliefs about education. These statements should cover several areas including children and developmental growth, teaching and learning at all levels but most particularly in relation to the position opening, education and its role in the community and society, standards, reform, assessment, and an educator's knowledge and relationship with legal issues and other educational and societal communities and values. The applicant should be able to write and verbally describe these beliefs in a manner that communicates commitment and sincerity. These beliefs should be second nature and so totally internalized that they guide everything that follows.

After the applicant is confident that she can articulate a personal philosophy, she should reduce that set of beliefs down to a series of simple and briefly worded (five words or less) tenets. This makes it easier to apply and communicate the belief system to oneself and in any interview situation.

For purposes of preparing for the interview, from these tenets the applicant should select *one tenet*, phrasing it in no more than five words. This tenet should be firmly in mind and heart—a profound belief. It should be a tenet that all questions and situations in the interview can be framed around.

Once internalized, this concept can be applied to any situation, question, or hypothetical example; any question that may take the applicant by surprise; a topic where the applicant's background and knowledge may not be as strong; or a time when the applicant simply needs more time to think and process information into a response. Each person should choose the one tenet that works best for her. Some examples are what's best for kids, standards, academic achievement through developmentally appropriate practices (and be able to cite some of these practices), the whole child, differentiation, reading as the common denominator, and equality of opportunity and services. There are many tenets that can be used in this way; however, the applicant must choose the one that works best and is a core value for her.

With a belief system firmly in mind and heart and a single tenet selected, one that will provide a common denominator for all topics and situations, the applicant is ready for the next step in preparing for the interview.

Preparation

Ideally, a candidate's philosophy will need only fine-tuning. This next step in the process will require some time and effort, especially if this is a first-time interview or an interview for a new position, or this is the first application of the preparation process. After the first time, it requires only updating and review.

Some applicants have extensive background and will have little trouble with these next two sections: *preparation* and *practice*. Other applicants will have things to learn in order to be thoroughly versed and prepared for both the interview and the job (because, really, isn't the application and interview only a glimpse into doing the job itself?). The applicant must trust that putting the time into this front-end work will pay off throughout the process. This work should begin two or more weeks in advance, especially when it is applied for the first time. Here are the steps:

1. Write down (yes, *write*) every question you can think of regarding the position for which you are applying in the areas of educational issues and educational content. Some typical examples might be today's standards, Common Core, instructional leadership, high-stakes testing in balance with teaching the whole child, staff supervision, data-based school improvement, relations with parents and the community, specific issues related to grade levels and schools (middle school concepts and programs, high school reform and scheduling options, elementary looping and blended classes, reading programs at the elementary level)—the list goes on quite extensively. Don't be deterred by how long your list of questions and issues becomes, and don't feel it must be completed at one sitting. New things will occur to you as you think through your list. Initiate conversations with other administrators and colleagues with questions such as, "What do you think are the significant educational issues of today?" to stimulate the introduction of additional topics to your list. But most important, be exhaustive. An administrator who was an ex-speech teacher and debate coach states, "I cannot overstate the reality that *confidence arises from thorough preparation*." It's better to know too much for an interview than too little. Even if something for which you have prepared is not a part of the interview, *it will be* in carrying out the responsibilities of the position!
2. After you have developed your list of questions, write (yes, *write*) the answers. As if it were an essay test, write everything you know about each question on your list. Do so using complete sentences. This begins the mental internalization, reinforcement, and recall of your already considerable knowledge base, and begins to prompt

you into thinking and placing that information in complete sentences, something you usually don't do when merely thinking of an answer or subject points. After all, in the interview, that is how you will have to communicate—in complete sentences. You do not communicate in phrases or thoughtful glimpses into the mind.
3. After you have written the answers to your questions, you will be able to pinpoint topics about which you need more information. Some of your questions may contain topics about which your experience and background are limited. There may be areas in which you won't have adequate information should they arise in an interview. So research them. Contact the State Department. Read articles on selected topics. Search the Internet. Contact a colleague, mentor, or specialist. Whatever method you use, research areas about which you realize you have inadequate information. Don't just hope they won't be a part of your interview. Inevitably, they will be, or you will unnecessarily worry that they might. Remember, the purpose here is to reduce anxiety, not create new situations that might generate it.
4. After you have completed your research, go back to your written answers and read them against this newly acquired information. Rewrite any question where you may have new information, incorporating that new information into your answer. Write an answer to any question that you have left blank. At this point, you should have written answers to all questions on your list from step 1.
5. Read your answers over until you are sure of the content. After a while, you will begin to anticipate the answers as soon as you read the question and the information. The response will become second nature to you.
6. Condense all the information in your answers onto a single 8 1/2 x 11 page. Use blocks to surround ideas. Highlight phrases and key words. Draw arrows. Do whatever makes sense to you, but condense the information.

Practice

1. After you have put all the information on one sheet, keep it handy and within reach. Throughout the days that follow, take out your sheet and glance at it, or shut your eyes and place your finger on a random spot to select a topic for practice. Once you have identified a topic, practice reciting the answer in your head and out loud—in complete sentences.
2. *At least* 50 percent of your practice should be out loud, and a part of that "out loud" time should be in front of a mirror. You may even want to tape yourself. Things are different when you speak and hear them than when you think them. Speaking is slower, for

one thing. It takes longer to talk than to think. Get used to the sounds and the pauses, to hearing how you phrase sentences, to how you sound and react when something happens in the interview that causes you to hesitate on a sentence or word. It is reassuring to know how you sound and react so that, when something happens in the interview, you do not become distracted by your performance or lose your chain of thought.

3. As much as possible, respond directly, succinctly, and specifically to any question using your preparation information. Do not use one question as the springboard to recite everything you know. Be thorough, knowledgeable, and most important, *to the point*. This is a key skill for any administrator. How many times, in answer to your question, have you thought "Just answer the question?" Sometimes in an interview, a question will be asked or a hypothetical situation will be presented for which you have not directly prepared, or one that needs some additional clarification or definition or direction. In that case . . .

4. Think back to the *single tenet* concept in the philosophy section. As you prepare, ask yourself some questions and don't use your carefully planned preparation in answering them. Pretend you don't know the answer and respond to the question framing your answer around your single tenet. Repeat the question incorporating your belief, your tenet. Rephrase it, moving it into the terminology and concept of the belief, your tenet. Do this orally, taking the time to settle into a response using information from another answer or describing how your philosophy might guide your approach in responding to a hypothetical example. Add details or examples of variables to the question as you prepare to answer the question. Practice this approach and technique and feel comfortable with it. This step is critical to approaching an interview situation with a sense of security and confidence. When thoroughly practiced, nothing that might happen in the interview will confuse or stymie you.

5. Now reduce all your 8 1/2 x 11 information onto a single note card. These are your last refresher notes. By this time, the interview will be a day or two away, and you will have written, rewritten, and practiced your responses in the context of an exhaustive list of questions and topics. Your command of the knowledge will be secured through your writing, research, thinking, and speaking. You will have reinforced the information, as you have had to condense it. This last refresher note is simply something at which to glance and to refer as you make final preparations for the interview and will, along with your confidence in placing *any* issue in the context of your tenet, provide for you a sense of confidence that you can handle anything in your interview.

By following the steps in the model described above, two significant and important outcomes emerge. First, everyone desires to do well in an interview situation, both to place himself in the best possible position to secure the job to which he is applying and to be comfortable with the content and qualifications for the administrative role.

Second, once an applicant is successful in obtaining the administrative position for which she applies, she then has to successfully do the job. By preparing thoroughly for the interview, the applicant is also undergoing a thorough and relevant preparation for the position itself.

One last note—that refresher sheet? The single 8 1/2 x 11 page with your condensed information? Save it. With any administrative position comes myriads of speeches, both formal and informal. This handy framework can be used to shape speeches or presentations that come your way. Or you may be faced with another interview sometime in the future, and this sheet can work as the starting point in your preparation.

EIGHTEEN
Time to Reflect and Recharge

Valuing Vacations

A house framer who labors every day is tired at the end of the day. The body needs rest, and after that rest the framer is refreshed and ready to work again. So too the mind needs rest. With the long hours, early mornings, and late nights, it is difficult to engage in outlets that let the mind rest or simply change gears—except for sleep, which many times is disturbed and interrupted by leftover thoughts and pressures.

During a regularly scheduled administrators' meeting, the superintendent of a large district told the administrative staff, "We want you to take your vacations. You work hard and under heavy expectations. We want you to get away and come back rested, refreshed, and invigorated."

The work of leading a school and the responsibilities for students, staff, and programs can be consuming. Educational leaders work hard. They work long hours, and at times they work under very stressful conditions. They are expected to be knowledgeable about and attentive to multiple tasks, programs, policies and law, and multiple aspects of the organization and its constituencies, all while being mindful of the mission of education. It can be exhausting. Without outlets, the work effects begin to compound, and even the most exemplary leader can be vulnerable to decreasing effectiveness, illness, or depression.

An effective administrator will calmly and efficiently respond to circumstances as they present themselves and as their individual and institutional needs surface. To be able to do so, it is important to take time to recharge. This usually comes in the form of a vacation. It allows for:

- Thinking without interruption
- Directing energies toward something completely different from the issues from the office, school, district, or association—temporarily leaving behind the challenges and work
- Getting out from under the constant multiple stimuli

Vacations provide for a diversion from the consuming issues and time required for leadership in education. The issues and challenges won't disappear, but after a break, when the administrator returns to the office, he is ready to approach them with renewed energy.

A principal once told his assistants that he needed some time away from the school. "Two weeks at the minimum," he said. "It takes about a week to quit thinking about the place and then several days of relaxing or playing. Then about three days before returning I start thinking about school again, getting ready to come back. Yup, two weeks minimum."

That lesson was so ingrained in one of those assistants that many years later, when he was president of a national association, he gave the same advice and expectation to the executive director. He went so far as to chart out her upcoming events and help her schedule a two-week break.

With technology, phones, and devices, it is increasingly difficult to "get away" entirely, although a recent film and television advertisements asks, "When did it become a source of guilt to leave work early?" Technology is a given; nonetheless, vacations are important and they should be viewed as something more than a luxury. There will always be something to do, and there will always be someone or something that expects or demands attention. Other personnel will step up to address immediate concerns, and scheduling can accommodate most other people and issues. Things will wait.

Leadership is a gestalt. Everything affects everything. Vacations are an element of that gestalt, one that can have a positive effect.

NINETEEN
The Gestalt of Leadership

Here is one more definition:

Complex: A whole made up of complicated or interrelated parts (*Webster's*).

How better to describe leadership and the act of leading than by recognizing that it is a phenomenon affected and brought together by multiple factors, making it complex. Everything about leadership—the leaders, the environment, the conditions, and the issues—come together, affect each other, and create a dynamic "whole." A gestalt.

Leadership is multifaceted in analysis and sometimes difficult in practice because it is complex.

In the context of education, leadership is guided by a set of values and beliefs. Those who are or aspire to be leaders in education should know those values and beliefs. They should be knowledgeable about the elements of instructional leadership as well as be able to manage the resources with which they are provided. They should know the science (the research, information, and knowledge base) of many facets of leadership. Effective, exemplary administrative leaders then demonstrate the art—the appropriate and successful applications of that research and knowledge.

Leadership comes in many forms. One of those is a formal, designated leader. Others provide leadership in a situational and more informal, albeit influential way.

Sometimes when the complex attributes of leadership come together, the exemplary leader—one with training, experience, and a set of innate skills and talents that provides capacity—emerges.

Every leader, formal or informal, confronts issues and is required to make decisions. There are models for assessing who participated in the decision-making process. There are models to analyze issues when considering the alternatives, ways that provide a conscious, careful, and cerebral approach to making the decision.

All of these complexities come together and form the gestalt, or the whole, of leadership.

Conclusion

The origin of *The Art and Science of Leading: What Effective Administrators Understand* was revealed in the preface. It began during a lunch discussion when one of three friends brought up the topic of a recent project, one in which another of the friends had been engaged. The discussion led to these questions: "As you conducted the searches for the executive director position, where did you find the best candidates? Where did they come from? What is the best preparation for a position like that?"

This conclusion returns to these questions.

Executive director candidates will come from many backgrounds. While there are exceptions (military, business), the two most usual backgrounds from which they come are education and associations. Given the responsibilities and tasks of an executive director, perhaps the best preparation for the position is as a superintendent of schools, although an incumbent association or affiliate leader also will have the background and exposure to the role and thus have similar experiences and preparation.

Although the superintendency may provide the best preparation for an executive director position, few superintendents apply, and salary may be an important factor. Many superintendents, almost all from large districts, are at a high point in salary and compensation. Many associations, in particular the one for which the search was conducted that prompted this conclusion, cannot offer or match the salary of a successful superintendent.

Leadership attributes, skills, background, and knowledge requirements are common to any leadership position. However, associations are different from schools and school districts and require different applications of those leadership abilities. Although there are leadership overlap and similarities, there are also differences.

The elements of leadership apply to all of these leadership positions in schools and associations. When hiring, it is desirable to have a candidate slate where every one of the candidates possesses all of the characteristics, skills, and elements of an exemplary leader. However, the final selection will always depend on who applies, what group of people make up the candidate pool, and from what group candidates must be selected.

In the case of selecting an executive director, every person involved in the selection process, officially and unofficially, has an ideal candidate in mind as the process begins. Everyone is looking for someone whose performance exhibits, to a high degree, everything and more that was included in the preceding chapters.

The candidate pool *sometimes* contains that person; however, rarely is that the case. When the list of candidates is finalized, the ideal person may not be on the list, and the person who "has everything" may not be among the final options. This requires that the selection committee use its best judgment and make a selection from the candidates who *do* apply. The selection committee and board will have to determine which one of the candidates most closely matches the characteristics and needs of the association.

One thread that runs through both school systems and associations is *a sense of mission.*

A sense of mission should hold priority and bring together any differences in style, structure, or required leadership in all levels of schooling. No leader at any level or in any role should ever lose sight of the mission, which is to realize the education of all the children. In association work, too, the mission must be foremost. The way associations work to realize the mission is through an ongoing commitment to provide service to all members of the organization.

Another commonality to both school systems and associations is the need for developing and implementing strategic planning. Any organization must have a vision and goals and specific plans to realize that vision. It is the responsibility of the superintendent or the executive director to ensure that strategic planning is part of the core work of the organization. More specifically, the following list describes the responsibilities of the superintendent or the executive director:

- Have a vision for the association and know how to move the organization toward realizing the vision.
- Understand that the board has the overarching responsibility and accountability and that the executive director is a representative of the board.
- Understand how to effectively manage the environment of being a representative, not the ultimate authority of the association. Understand how to help bring about an "empowerment" balance.
- Work with an elected board and officers who represent perspectives from around the country or even the world. The executive director's work includes:
  - Sharing the vision and including the board in developing the vision
  - Helping the president and board do their work, including their fiduciary responsibilities; self-imposed tasks and responsibilities; and other constitutional, policy, and mission responsibilities
  - Supporting the board, keeping the board informed

- Knowing when to lead and when to follow
- Project an appropriate professional image of the association to others, including other associations, policy makers, and constituent groups
- Represent the association and advocate for its mission
- Have business background, abilities, and knowledge—experiences that reflect a successful record of providing a solid revenue stream and a balanced budget
- Manage the resources: human, financial, and philosophical
- Generate an income and revenue stream through membership, publications, grants, or investments
- Balance the budget: expenditures to revenue
- Supervise the staff

Comparing the roles and responsibilities of the executive director to those of all school administrators, with all things considered and in an ideal world (assuming the candidate pool presents a list of many qualified candidates from different backgrounds and with different experiences), a superintendent would seem to be the educational leader who has the most similar and common sets of experience in preparation for the position of executive director. Consider the following responsibilities of a superintendent which would qualify him for the position of executive director:

- Must have a vision for the district, balance income with expenditures, and represent the district.
- Must work with a board, as does an executive director. Other administrators do not have that direct and very political contact with elected policy makers.
- Must work *through people*, not through dictates. He will have immediate supervision and authority over the district office staff. Other than those in the district office, the rest of the staff, licensed and classified employees in each school, is directly supervised by the school principals. For the superintendent to be effective, he must work through the principals.
- May have supervisory authority over principals; however, unless there is malfeasance, unacceptable performance, or a real potential for dismissal, the superintendent does not dictate behavior and certainly cannot "run the school." Similarly, an executive director may hold sway over the association staff but cannot dictate or behave authoritatively in regard to the president, board, members, affiliates, other influential members, or sponsors or partners—many of whom have direct impact on students.

- Must live within the policies enacted by the board and guided by law. An executive director must likewise conduct the business and work of an association within the policies enacted by its board.

When considering which position provides the most appropriate preparation for an executive director position, a major difference between a superintendent and principals, or other administrators, is that the superintendent must be skilled at and will have experience working with boards.

DIFFERENCES

An association must generate its own "community" and its own resources. These are provided to a school district, but an association must generate its own.

In the settings of formal schooling there will be three ongoing "givens." These givens ensure a degree of security and predictability, including a continuing membership base and some degree of financial support:

- A community
- Students
- A district

The same is not true in association work. A school district will have a staff and ongoing, identifiable, and consistent communities. Associations are membership based, and if the members do not see immediate and measurable results, they will not join. Additionally, the affiliate organizations, leaders, members, and partnerships will change, sometimes regularly.

A school district will go on, for better or for worse. However, the continued existence of an association depends on several factors:

- Its relevance
- The services and voice it provides
- A continuous and always changing income stream
- The activities of the board and the integrity, influence, charisma, and behavior of the staff, particularly the executive director

To generate those communities and resources to remain in existence, an association must be relevant, responsive, honest, and solvent, or it will cease to exist. And it should.

As undesirable as it may be, a school district can be irrelevant, unresponsive, and dishonest (in different ways), yet be solvent and continue on. The difference between predictability and self-generation demands some very unique experiences and abilities from an executive director compared to those of a school administrator. The executive director of an association has the same expectations, responsibilities, and roles in leadership but has additional ones that are not expected of a school administrator, building administrator, or district office superintendent.

VOLUNTEERS

The work of volunteers in a school district is very different from the work of volunteers in an association. The existence, survival, strength, and continued relevance of an association depend on the work of volunteers and leaders from a wider constituency. Working with volunteers is, at times, quite difficult and tricky:

- Volunteers may not have a wide range of understanding or abilities.
- It is complex to resolve certain issues when personalities become an issue rather than the issue itself.
- Associations depend on people being willing to contribute their time and money because they believe in the mission of the association. A school district does not require volunteers for its work.
- A staff is "provided" to a school district, and it carries out the work for a salary and within contract and legal parameters.

The pool of volunteers in an association depends on the association's relevance and its ability to attract and involve them, convincing them to be a part of the association and affiliating with its mission and giving them relevant, important tasks. Executive directors live with this responsibility, and must direct resources and programs to continually make the association attractive. School district administrators do not have that same requirement, or at least not to the same level or with the same consequences.

All positions in a school district are appointed and hired by the board. Being hired implies remuneration, and the positions exist in an organizational, hierarchical structure.

In school districts or schools, volunteers may work side by side with teachers and principals on some district-level projects, such as an antidrug campaign, a budget election, or a curriculum review. It is helpful to have volunteers; however, the district would continue without them. In fact, some districts or schools within larger districts have no volunteers at all.

Throughout the rest of the organization, the staff is supervised and can be sanctioned at various levels, even leading to dismissal. *Volunteers are rarely, if ever, sanctioned or asked to leave.*

A school district board of directors is another example of volunteers in a district. They are unpaid positions, and the board members have broad responsibilities for policy, budgets, and hiring/supervising the superintendent. This is similar to associations, although changes in laws and funding have somewhat reduced the autonomy and influence of school boards. Nonetheless, they are highly influential, particularly with the superintendent whom they hire and evaluate. A school board also has the legal responsibility to approve and oversee the district budget, though personnel and fixed costs, along with legislative mandates, make this responsibility less significant than it once was.

In school districts, the community patrons are the electorate. The electorate is static and provided. There are typically no sanctions for school district volunteers except in extreme cases as established by law or by electoral replacement at the next election.

As with schools, hired staff members are supervised by the leader in the association, usually the executive director. A staff member can be sanctioned or dismissed.

Volunteers elected to an association board have legal and mission responsibilities. An elected president has organizational influence, using the position to work with the executive director, staff, and other members of the board, including formal and informal leadership responsibilities to the full board. The president also has control over processes such as agenda setting, establishing new initiatives and discarding past ones, and forging a vision for the association.

In a school district, administrative leaders are hired. Selection is based on experience, skills, past performance, and background. In an association, the executive director and staff are hired based on the same general criteria. However, the president of an association, a significant and influential leader with many responsibilities and needed skills in the organization, is elected. As with all elections, the president, well intentioned and with leadership skills and potential, may be elected based on factors other than being the most qualified for the position.

Typically, no one or no position has oversight over the president, although the president must live within the constitutional and legal parameters of the association office. Impeachment and recall are available and could be used for gross malfeasance or legal violations, but these two sanction options are seldom applied.

Other association volunteers are committee chairs and members who serve for terms and are rarely removed after appointment, though technically they could be.

Advisers and mentors usually serve unofficially as long as they have value and are needed. They typically have no power except that of their advice, position, and ability. They too are instrumental volunteers and must be considered by an association.

One of the questions for both the district and association is, "How do you sanction a volunteer?" Staff members may be dismissed. Volunteers are another matter:

- A national association has hired staff members. They are hired, supervised by, accountable to, and dismissed by the executive director. These staff members are not hired by the board, so they are not necessarily accountable to it. Staff members are not limited to national associations. Some state associations are big and solvent enough to have a staff.
- National associations could not exist without a hired staff. The staff members, as in a school district, do the work.
- School district staffs are all hired by the board and supervised by other staff but may be dismissed only by the board after receiving a recommendation from the superintendent or other supervisory personnel.
- Volunteer work in associations, particularly national associations, and in contract to the school districts is critical to the association's operations. There are legal and constitutional requirements for board members (volunteers) such as a strict fiduciary responsibility.
- The volunteers are instrumental in the ongoing relevance of association products and the association itself. Some other examples of volunteer work in associations include:
    - Board members: elected by the membership and set policy and direction, hire and supervise the executive director, approve the budget, and ensure financial solvency
    - President and other officers: elected by the membership, work with executive director
    - Task force chairs and members: appointed by the president or board
    - Standing committee chairs and members: appointed by the president or board
    - Advisers/mentors to executive director and/or officers: may be informal but their involvement is necessary, if only to keep them involved and interested

Volunteers have a significant impact on association viability and survival. As an association grows in members and influence and adds alternative income revenues, the association will begin to have less reliance and dependency on volunteerism except for complying with the association constitution and legal requirements. When that evolves, the executive director and staff take on more responsibility and leadership for the association, causing it to look more like a school district. The board continues to be influential, but other volunteer work becomes less critical.

As in school districts, there is little, if any provision, for sanctioning a volunteer. Not so critical in a school district, it can cause difficulties for an association. For example, if the staff is overloaded with multiple tasks or does not have a specific, needed knowledge set, the association may involve a volunteer to take leadership and work on a significant project, working closely with a staff member. Staff members can be sanctioned by the executive director; however, the volunteer has no formal supervisory authority overseeing her work. As a volunteer is not included in the official organizational structure and does not receive remuneration, there is limited supervisory influence and no provision for sanction. All is well as long as the volunteer and staff agree on direction and process and they get along. When they don't, the association leader (executive director) must make a decision and consider:

- His loyalty to the staff on one hand and the volunteer on the other
- Whether the product and outcomes of the product/activity are sufficient to warrant continuation, even though there is volunteer/staff conflict
- What the implications to staff are if the volunteer prevails
- What the implications are for volunteerism and the ramifications from this volunteer's supporters if the staff members prevail (this was discussed to a larger degree in chapter 11: Analysis Prior to Decision Making)

On one hand, in a school district, an issue such as this may never reach the superintendent, and if it does it poses only slight political discomfort. On the other hand, in an association, which relies on its volunteers for work, growth, support, and membership, it could be a much larger issue with further-reaching consequences.

FISCAL AND LEGAL KNOWLEDGE

A superintendent must have budgeting, building, and monitoring skills and knowledge. Many districts have a staff member who is an expert on monetary matters—a chief financial officer (CFO). The CFO may or may not be an educator. The CFO does have financial expertise, experience, and training.

An executive director must have much more knowledge of financial issues than a superintendent does. The executive director needs a wider range of skills because she has less access to others. An association usually has to pay for financial expertise via consultants or accountants. The executive director also must be aware of IRS rules, nonprofit regulations and restrictions, and other ramifications of her financial decisions.

An executive director must also know the legal ramifications on a much wider range of compliance issues, including administrative operations, human relations, and contract negotiation. Most districts have personnel to address these issues, whereas most associations do not have specialists in these areas.

The mission and content of associations may be different, but the work is similar among them, which allows for moving from one association to another if the executive director is an exemplary leader, smart and motivated, and willing to focus on a new mission.

THE NATIONAL MIDDLE SCHOOL ASSOCIATION SEARCH

In the search for an executive director for the National Middle School Association (NMSA), there was a contingent in the membership who stressed the importance of subject matter. These members, in some cases particularly important historical figures, were exerting influence to make sure the person who was ultimately selected was well versed and experienced in middle level education. The board considered this but reached a different conclusion.

Smart and motivated exemplary leaders can and will learn. For example, coming from many years of high school experience as a teacher, counselor, and vice principal, a school administrator saw that middle schools were gaining in recognition and attention. He thought that there was opportunity for school reform and change. He moved to the principalship of a middle school. In a very short time, he became fully versed in the issues and research regarding young adolescents and middle schooling and a leader in both education and middle level association work.

Another example: A successful, exemplary leader served as the executive director for an association. Seeking a change, she applied for an executive director position at another association, one with a different mission, focus, and knowledge base. She accepted the offered position, quickly learned the knowledge base, and committed to the mission. She was highly successful in her new position, although she did not initially have the content background.

With the belief that exemplary, motivated, smart leaders will learn, the NMSA board and search committee determined that too often the desire to have subject matter expertise took unacceptable precedence over the leadership skills necessary for effective association leadership. The NMSA position was posted as Middle Level Experience *desirable* (not required).

Also in relation to the NMSA search, while the position did not call strictly for a businessperson (though a businessperson would not have been ruled out), the association's financial requirements were such that it would be desirable to be run in a businesslike way. Financial management was a high priority. Executives from other associations had the background experiences that lent themselves to financial management. So too do superintendents, though to a lesser extent. In the NMSA search, there were no applicants who were incumbent superintendents.

The leadership of one year may not be the leadership needed the next year. Associations change. Their needs change. They are different from year to year. So too are leaders different, with different skills and abilities. Finding the match is key to a successful search.

Regardless of preparation and from where a candidate comes, the leadership skills that the candidate brings may or may not match the needs of the association at the time of selection. Just as with schools and districts, the candidate not hired today may be exactly the candidate needed to fit the needs of the position and association tomorrow. Associations are different; they are different year to year. So too are leaders. Finding the match is key to the success of filling these positions.

SUMMARY

- There are key elements to exemplary leadership: experiential, learned, and innate.
- Exemplary leaders will always be successful — anywhere.
- Smart, intelligent, and motivated leaders can and will learn what they need to know to be successful.
- There are different skill sets between an educational leader and an association leader, though there is overlap between the two.
- It is highly desirable for a superintendent to have education experience; however, both a district superintendent and an association leader, if they are exemplary leaders, can learn and be successful without it.
- It is desirable for an association executive director to have experience as a superintendent in education.

Appendix 1

STRATEGIC PLAN OUTLINE

Strategic planning: The following is a sample. It is an outline of a strategic plan, though only partially completed. The final plan will be much longer and more thorough and complete—much more detailed and specific.

This is intended as a starting point and model for those looking to develop a strategic plan. Completing this plan would require that the planners individualize to their own projects, school, and personnel as exemplified in the third section of this example, Specific Plans to Implement the Ideas and Goals.

Vision

The middle school will be a place where:

- Students and staff are happy and look forward to coming to school every day.
- Students and staff feel safe and valued.
- Every staff member is knowledgeable about and enjoys working with young adolescents.
- Learning is interesting and relevant to everyday life and student goals. Teaching is geared toward student interests, abilities, and achievement levels.
- Instructional programs and all other programs are research based and appropriate to the age group.
- Individual staff members are continually growing and being successful.

Ideas and Goals to Realize the Vision

- Conduct efficacy and safety assessments.
- Assess staff knowledge about and desire to work with young adolescents. One hundred percent of the staff should know the developmental characteristics, be knowledgeable about instructional theory and practice to address those characteristics, and enjoy working with this age group.
- Assess classroom instruction to determine the relevance to students and the community life.

- Research sources that provide information and program recommendations for schools serving young adolescents.

Specific Plans to Implement the Ideas and Goals

- Counselors conduct focus groups with students and staff. Specific plans needed to complete this step:
    - Inform staff members at a faculty meeting. Share with them the goal and provide a preview of some of the related activities. Share the timeline and topics. Principal with one counselor at October 10 meeting.
    - Prepare counselors to conduct the groups by having book discussions during scheduled sessions. Principal selects book, schedules sessions, and conducts discussion. Completed by November 5.
    - Randomly select and schedule students and staff. Counselor's responsibility with support from administrators. Draft schedule presented to leadership team at December 10 meeting.
    - Counselors complete focus groups. They generate patterns, conclusions, and summaries for discussion at January 31 leadership team meeting.
    - Leadership team finalizes conclusions and establishes goals, along with respective goals to address results (January 31–February 10). Share with faculty, solicit input from faculty, finalize new ideas and goals (February 15 meeting).
- Increase classroom observations. Focus on specific items such as teacher/student relationships and teaching strategies that are appropriate to the age group. Specific plans needed to implement this step:
    - Discuss with all teacher supervisors the desired "look fors" during observations and day-to-day interactions and observations. Finalize. Principal initiates discussion, calls meeting. Completed by June 30 and ready for the coming year.
    - Meet with supervisors monthly to compare observations, both formal and informal. Identify staff members who are appropriately placed, committed but need additional support and information, and would prefer to be placed elsewhere. Completed by March 15. Principal schedules the meeting, supervisors participate.
    - Principal sets staffing goals based on discussions and finalized list. The goals will involve working with the personnel department (transfers, leaves, etc.), counseling staff members (helping them move, setting or imposing individual goals

working with individuals to identify pathways to successful teaching, etc.), providing support and professional development (all-school and individual). It also involves a hiring strategy, developed by the principal and implemented with every staff vacancy.
- Counseling and meeting with staff members also addresses the goal of individual staff development and growth. This is ongoing. Meet formally according to supervision schedule. Continue to discuss the individual's future plans and dreams. Assist with goal setting to realize those plans. Have informal discussions with individuals in their work spaces and in the office.
- Ask each individual where she sees herself in five years. If individuals are unsure, advise them on putting together a plan. Support that plan, help create activities, and provide resources to help each staff person realize the goals of the plan.
- Conduct a middle school assessment study. Principal will research and select an instrument by January 10. The assessment will be conducted in March. All staff members are involved. It will be coordinated and carried out by the principal whose responsibility and oversight it will be to initiate, schedule, and monitor progress. Support from leadership team. Results analyzed by April 1. Shared with staff (need to determine how to do this—faculty meeting or in small groups?). Results of the assessment, possible school goals discussed and finalized by leadership team. All staff has input, principal makes final determination based on results and staff discussions (May 20).

Appendix 2

NATIONAL ASSOCIATION OF SECONDARY SCHOOL PRINCIPALS' (NASSP) ASSESSMENT CENTER

The purpose of the NASSP Assessment Center is twofold: (1) The assessment center accurately diagnoses the presence and strength of skills to assist in selection and development. (2) The center forms skill awareness for effective practice and serves as a baseline diagnosis for individual development.

Selecting and developing the twenty-first-century principal provides a realistic job preview of the principalship. Participants engage in a one-day simulation consisting of six interrelated activities. The activities require participants to deal with accumulated paperwork, meet with an angry parent, conference with a teacher having performance problems, participate in a group meeting, prepare and deliver a formal oral presentation, and prepare a formal writing sample. In addition participants complete a biographical information form prior to their participation in the assessment center. A group of trained and certified assessors observe participants while they are completing the simulations. Assessors, utilizing computer software, record participant's behavior, describe the behavior, and classify the behavior into the appropriate skill. Behavior is recorded on ten skill dimensions that correlate with the Educational Leadership Policy Standards: ISLLC 2008 Standards.

Educational Leadership

- *Setting instructional direction.* Implementing strategies for improving teaching and learning including putting programs and improvement efforts into action. Developing a vision and establishing clear goals; providing direction in achieving stated goals; encouraging others to contribute to goal achievement; securing commitment to a course of action from individuals and groups.
- *Teamwork.* Seeking and encouraging involvement of team members. Modeling and encouraging the behaviors that move the group to task completion. Supporting group accomplishment.
- *Sensitivity.* Perceiving the needs and concerns of others; dealing tactfully with others in emotionally stressful situations or in conflict. Knowing what information to communicate and to whom.

Relating to people of varying ethnic, cultural, and religious backgrounds.

Resolving Complex Problems

- *Judgment.* Reaching logical conclusions and making high-quality decisions based on available information. Giving priority and caution to significant issues. Seeking out relevant data, facts, and impressions. Analyzing and interpreting complex information.
- *Results orientation.* Assuming responsibility. Recognizing when a decision is required. Taking prompt action as issues emerge. Resolving short-term issues while balancing them against long-term objectives.
- *Organizational ability.* Planning and scheduling one's own and the work of others so that resources are used appropriately. Scheduling flow of activities; establishing procedures to monitor projects. Practicing time and task management; knowing what to delegate and to whom.

Communication

- *Oral communication.* Clearly communicating. Making oral presentations that are clear and easy to understand.
- *Written communication.* Expressing ideas clearly in writing; demonstrating technical proficiency. Writing appropriately for different audiences.

Developing Self and Others

- *Development of others.* Teaching, coaching, and helping others. Providing specific feedback based on observations and data.
- *Understanding own strengths and weaknesses.* Understanding personal strengths and weaknesses. Taking responsibility for improvement by actively pursuing developmental activities. Striving for continual learning.

After participants complete the one-day simulation, the assessor team builds a composite report of the participant's performance describing the presence of strengths and weaknesses and identifying developmental needs. A computer-generated final report is delivered to the participant in a one-on-one feedback session a week to ten days after the simulation.

References

Barnlund, D., and F. Haiman. (1960). *Dynamics of discussion*. Boston: Houghton Mifflin Company, The Riverside Press.

Besag, V. E. (1989). *Bullies and victims in schools: A guide to understanding and management*. Buckingham, England: Open University Press.

Cain, S. (2013). *Quiet: The power of introverts in a world that can't stop talking*. New York: Broadway Paperbacks.

Canole, M., and M. Young. (2013). *Standards for educational leaders: An analysis*. Washington, DC: Council of Chief State School Officers. Retrieved from http://www.ccsso.org/Documents/Analysis%20of%20Leadership%20Standards-Final-070913-RGB.pdf.

The Council of Chief State School Officers (CCSSO). (2008). *Educational leadership policy standards: ISLLC 2008*. Retrieved from http://www.ccsso.org/Documents/2008/Educational_Leadership_Policy_Standards_2008.pdf.

Collins English Dictionary (19th ed.). (2009). New York: Harper Collins & Sons and Company.

Dictionary.com. (2014). Retrieved from http://www.dictionary.reference.com.

G and C Merriman, eds. (1971). *Webster's Seventh New Collegiate Dictionary*. Chicago: The Lakeside Press.

Gallup/SRI Principal Perceiver Interview Guide, Form A (4th ed.). (1979). Lincoln, NE: Selection Research, Inc.

Hoerr, T. R. (2007). What is instructional leadership? *Educational Leadership*, 65(4), 84–85.

Kozol, J. (1991). *Savage inequities: Children in America's schools*. New York: Crown Publishing Group.

Letterman, D. Interview with Donald Trump [Television series episode]. In *The late show with David Letterman*. New York. Aired October 17, 2013.

Quick, J. (2015, August 27). Dansby Swanson is out to change the world. *The Oregonian*.

Simon, P. (1968). "The Boxer." [Recorded by Paul Simon & Art Garfunkel]. On *Live 1969* [record] Long Beach, CA: Columbia Records (1969).

Tyre, P. (2015, September 27). How the school principal's job has changed. *Christian Science Monitor* and *The Hechinger Report*. Available at http://www.csmonitor.com/USA/Education/2015/0927/How-the-school-principal-s-job-has-changed.

U.S. Department of Education, National Center for Education Statistics. (2014, March). *Condition of America's Public School Facilities*. Retrieved from http://nces.ed.gov/pubs2014/2014022.pdf. This report provides national estimates on the condition of public school facilities. The study presented in this report collected information about the condition of public school facilities in the 2012–2013 school year.

About the Authors

Peter Lorain has held many positions in education: high school teacher, counselor, and vice principal; middle school principal; district director of high schools/middle schools; and district director for human resources. He is a past president of the National Middle School Association, now the Association for Middle Level Education (AMLE). He has chaired many AMLE committees and task forces and conducted numerous strategic planning sessions with state affiliate organizations. His consulting work is with schools and districts nationwide and on topics that include school improvement, all elements of young adolescent and middle level education, strategic planning, and personnel issues. From 2009 to 2011, he served as transition chair for AMLE, a position that bridged the time between a departing and newly hired executive director, working with the AMLE staff and board of trustees. In the transition role, he conducted two executive director searches for that association.

Gary Sehorn is currently an associate professor in the School of Education at George Fox University, Oregon. He has been a social studies teacher, middle school vice principal and principal, high school assistant principal, and K–12 administrator for curriculum instruction and assessment. Gary is an often published writer and presenter, holds memberships in several university and professional associations, and was appointed to the Curriculum Task Force for the National Middle School Association, now the Association for Middle Level Education.

Mike Scott is currently the superintendent of the Hillsboro, Oregon School District. His background includes positions as a teacher, middle school vice principal and principal, and assistant superintendent of human resources. He was the Oregon Middle Level Association's (OMLA) Principal of the Year, president of OMLA, and co-chair of the National Middle School Association's (now the Association for Middle Level Education) annual conference in Portland.

www.ingramcontent.com/pod-product-compliance
Lightning Source LLC
Chambersburg PA
CBHW021844220426
43663CB00005B/400